Legacy through the Lens

A STUDY OF MENDHAM ARCHITECTURE

By Janet W. Foster

Photographs by E. Kenneth Hoffman

Edited by Robert P. Guter

History by Jeanne Will

PUBLISHING DIRECTOR, RUTH HOEH SMITH

MENDHAM FREE PUBLIC LIBRARY

MENDHAM, N.J., 1986

PRINTED BY SCOTT PRINTING CORPORATION

This book is dedicated to

MARGARET and HUGO DeNEUFVILLE

for their enduring commitment to this community.

Publication of this book was aided by a grant from
the New Jersey Committee for the Humanities. The views
expressed herein are not necessarily those of the
New Jersey Committee for the Humanities.

Publication of this book was also aided by a grant from
the New Jersey Historical Commission.

Text set in Baskerville
by Fore Typesetting

**Printing contributed by Scott Printing Corporation,
Jersey City, New Jersey**

Library of Congress Catalog Card Number: 86-50972

ISBN 0-931661-005

Foreword

Throughout this book we have treated the present-day municipalities of Mendham Township and Mendham Borough as one entity, referred to as Mendham. Locating only those properties that can be seen from a public road, we have designated the area along State Highway 24 west of the Borough-Township line as Ralston, East and West Main Streets in the Township as Brookside, and East and West Main Streets in the Borough simply as Main Street.

Selecting and naming buildings from the rich stock of surviving historic architecture was a difficult process. We acknowledge that some of Mendham's oldest and most admired buildings are missing from these pages, and that most of the names given to houses will surprise both local readers and property owners. Some names were taken from local documents and deed research, but in most instances they come from the earliest map that indicates a property owner at the time a house was probably built or remodeled to the style discussed.

Buildings were selected to show the evolution of architecture from the first settlement to the present. In almost every instance buildings were chosen that retain their original architectural integrity, so that features characteristic of particular styles or types are highlighted. Architectural integrity should not be confused with a building's condition. Many beautifully maintained structures have lost their distinctive features because of additions and alterations, while those in disrepair may retain important stylistic elements, perhaps because of fortuitous neglect.

Projects of this scope happen because of the commitment of many people, each contributing their special talents and drawn together in their bond to the place they call home. We wish to give particular recognition to Virginia P. Blackketter, Ann Hartzell, J. D. Ketchum, Brigid Shanley Lamb, Syril T. Lebbad, O. M. Lee, Sarah Dean Link, Bonnie Lundberg, Terry Mulcahy, Marian Heath Mundy, Frances D. Pingeon, Linda C. Quinn, Diana Simon, Linda Steelman, Jeanne Will. We also want to thank all who graciously permitted their homes and businesses to be photographed, sometimes accommodating the photographer's return visits for a better angle or different lighting.

All original illustrations, including the Glossary, are by Ed Jaeckle.

This book is supported by grants from the New Jersey Committee for the Humanities, an affiliate of the National Endowment for the Humanities, and by the New Jersey Historical Commission. Additional funding has been provided by donations from more than one hundred families who live in Mendham Township and Mendham Borough, as well as substantial contributions from the Mendham Offices of Burgdorff Realtors and Schlott Realtors.

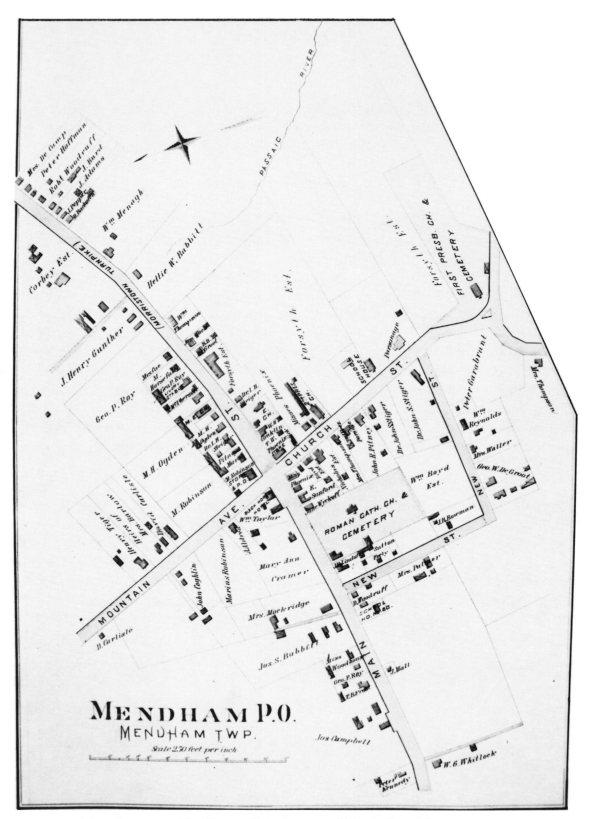

MENDHAM P.O.
MENDHAM TWP.

Scale 250 feet per inch

Courtesy of the Joint Free Public Library of Morristown and Morris Township.
1887 Map by E. Robinson.

PLATE 31

M O R R I S ⑥ PASSAIC ㉜

MENDHAM
TOWNSHIP.

Scale 3 inches per mile

UNION HILL DIST. No 64

WASHINGTON VALLEY DIST No 65

No. 62

BROOKSIDE DIST

Brookside

Washington Corner

WASHINGTON DIST No 63

M O R R I S

O L D B O O N T O N T U R N P I K E

㉔

Ralmoney

DIST. No. 61

DIST. No. 60

DIST. No. 59

Mendham P.O.

M E N D H A M

DIST No 58

M O U N T A I N

Roxibury

R A L S T O N T U R N P I K E

C H E S T E R

㉚

UNION DISTRICT

B E R N A R D S

LEIGH DIST No 57

Entered according to Act of Congress in the year 1887 by C Robinson in the Office of the Librarian of Congress at Washington D.C.

Contents

Preface

When I first got to know Mendham, almost twenty years ago, I was impressed by two things: its landmark buildings, like Hilltop Church and the Phoenix House, and its still rural landscape. The more I returned, the more I saw: Brookside's modest houses, and the Dismal Harmony green with skunk cabbage in spring; the Nesbitt Mill, snowbound and neglected, but full of potential; and Aaron Hudson, that elusive native son, whose buildings and "might-be" buildings continue to confound me.

I thought I knew Mendham, but Janet Foster and Ken Hoffman show me something new on almost every page, whether it's a building that had eluded me at the end of a long driveway or a familiar building cast in a fresh light. What their text and photos reveal is far more than landmarks. They see, and they show the reader, a place of unusual cohesiveness and variety. It's an environment that offers a special sense of place not because it is filled with spectacular or unique buildings, but because its buildings are "ordinary" in the best possible way. They are the houses, churches, mills and great estates that make up the connective tissue of larger historical events.

Since I first saw Mendham, a few things have happened for the worse, but the best still stands, in context. To a remarkable extent the usual plagues of aluminum siding, heedless road-widening and frenzied growth have bypassed the Borough and the Township. Such success is never accidental. I like to think that the people of Mendham realize they are not merely owners but custodians of a valuable cultural resource.

I hope this book opens even more eyes, so the things that inform and delight us in Mendham will be treated with care for another 200 years. I hope, too, that readers elsewhere will recognize in these pages reflections of their own special places. The battle to save New Jersey's historic architecture is far from over, and there are many Mendhams worth the fight.

Robert P. Guter
Morristown, 1986

History

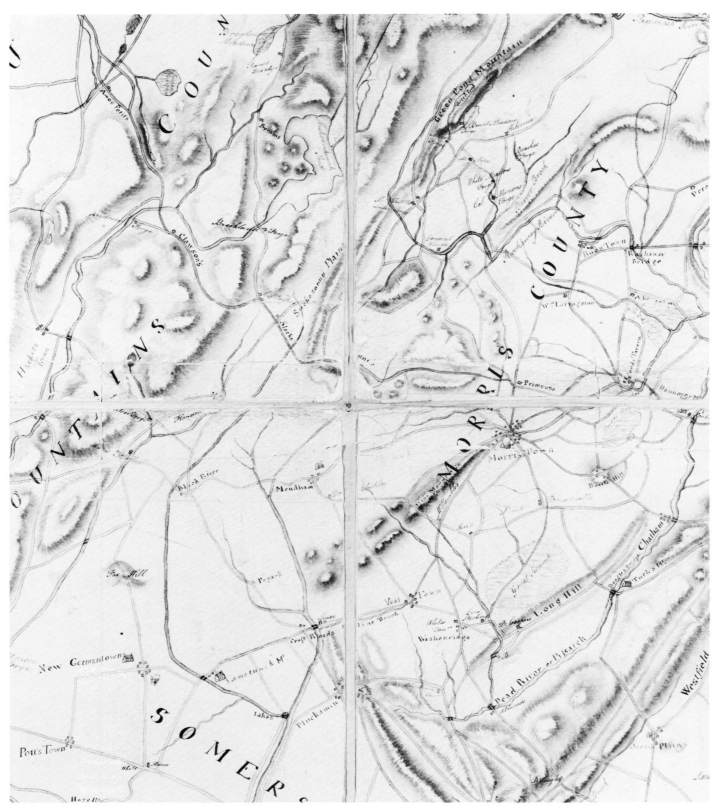

A section of a map entitled *Counties in New York Province Before 1779*.
Courtesy of the New York Historical Society, New York City.

A country village, slightly removed from the main stream of events, the formal history of Mendham is a brief one. The basic facts have been told and retold, often colored by legend, folklore, or family tradition. With few exceptions, the early residents of this predominantly agricultural community were men of deeds, not words, and of their lives we have the houses they built but few original accounts. Much has been pieced together from legal documents such as marriage and birth records or wills and inventories, however, the personal details which challenge our curiosity remain elusive.

The earliest recorded deed for the area was August 13, 1708, between the West Jersey Proprietors and a group of Minsi Indians of the Lenni Lenape tribe. Because they did not share the white man's concept of property ownership, these Indians were perhaps startled at a later date at the realization that they had given up their lands. However, in the absence of evidence to the contrary, it appears that relations between the first settlers and the local tribes were pleasant ones. There were one or more Indian villages within the boundaries of present day Mendham but their exact location has not been substantiated.

What is known is that in 1713, John Wills was deeded approximately 862 acres in Roxiticus (Rocksiticus) possibly in return for his services as surveyor to the West Jersey Proprietors. His father, Daniel Wills, had come to West Jersey from England in the ship "Kent" in 1677. Descendants of this family apparently did not settle on their land for another ten years, probably at the time of son James' marriage to Sarah Clement in 1724. The Wills' property extended on both sides of the Indian trail later known successively as King's Highway, the Washington Turnpike and State Highway 24. A small Wills' family graveyard can still be seen on the hill at the entrance to the Oak Knoll subdivision.

The region was gradually settled by families from New England and Long Island who were predominantly of Scotch and Irish Protestant ancestry. Others, who came by way of the Raritan and Passaic rivers through New Brunswick and Morristown, were mainly English. We have no evidence that they were drawn to this area by a specific religious or political conviction, but as farmers and tradespeople, were perhaps simply in search of a place where they could enjoy peace and prosperity. An early account of Mendham describes the area as:

> ". . . remarkably well drained and very fertile. All fruits, grains, berries and grapes natural to this latitude grow to great perfection and are exceedingly well flavored. Men and animals are healthy and longevity is the rule:"

The mountain view from Picatinny Road, still unmarred by many signs of civilization, reveals what early travelers may have seen to cause them to remain. The gentle rolling landscape is well wooded and watered by numerous springs and brooks, in earlier times a necessary source of power for small industries. A rumor of substantial iron ore deposits in the region gave further impetus to settlement.

The Mendham area was located near the disputed East/West Jersey boundary line and thus there was some influence on the early settlers from both the rigid, strict, Puritannical people of East Jersey and the more peaceable followers of William Penn. One hundred years ago, the Hon. S. B. Axtell wrote that:

> "The exceeding healthfulness of the climate has also probably contributed to moderate and purify the temperament of the inhabitants. The children born of healthful industrious and virtuous parents have naturally and cheerfully walked in the ways of virtue and the path of peace."

By the 1730's a small group of settlers had formed along India Brook in Roxiticus, later renamed Ralston after one of its prominent citizens. Soon a Meeting House was constructed on the hill just east of this location, to serve both the spiritual and temporal needs of the community. A larger settlement formed about one and one-half miles east and was established as the town center by the 1740's. Another settlement about four miles to the north east became the small village of Waterville, later renamed Brookside. In 1749, the entire area was incorporated by the Morris County Court, thus becoming one of the first townships in the county. The area which is now Chester separated and became an independent township in 1799 and Randolph, in 1805. What remained of Mendham Township formed a single unit until 1906 when the Borough was formed, as required by law, for the purpose of establishing a water system.

Among the early settlers in the region were Jacob Cook; Caleb Baldwin; Joseph Thompson, father of David; Ebenezer Condit; Henry Wick; and Jacob Drake and Levi Lewis, whose descendants still live in Mendham. Perhaps the most colorful among this group was Ebenezer Byram who came to the region in 1743 from Bridgewater, Massachusetts with his five sons and three daughters. A proprietor of the Black Horse Tavern, he was a leader in the community and served as Justice of the Peace and as a Major in the militia. He is credited with having named the area Mendham (Mendon, Mendum) after his ancestral village in England. His son Ebenezer married Abigail who was a direct descendant of Captain John Alden and his wife, Priscilla of "Mayflower" fame.

Another prominent local resident was Dr. Ebenezer Blachley who lived in the southern portion of the township. One of the founders of the New Jersey Medical Society, he ran a medical school in his home in which he trained five of his sons in the medical arts. Other settlers of particular note were Stephen Dod, a well known clockmaker, and Dr. Wm. Leddell Jr., another of Dr. Blachley's students.

James Pitney, an Englishman, purchased land about 1722. His descendants have occupied the homestead, known as Pitney Farms, since that date, and include several lawyers and judges prominent in New Jersey government. The only properties in the Mendham area clearly identified on a map drawn in the early

1750's for Lord Somerville are Pitney Farms and Dr. Blachley's house, presumably considered important landmarks.

By 1745, a doctrinal dispute had divided the Roxiticus meeting house and some members went west to build a house of worship in Chester, while others regrouped to build the Mendham church later known as Hilltop. The site chosen by Ebenezer Byram commands a panoramic view of the countryside, and the steeple of the current church, the fourth building to be constructed on the site, can be seen for miles around, reminding one of the importance of the religious element in the lives of these early settlers. It is interesting to note that in the first deed, dated November 25, 1747, for the property on which the original meeting house was built, the grant was made not to a sect or society but "unto the Congregation of Inhabitance of people that do or shall frequently meet together to worship God in that place . . . ."

The first pastor of the new church was Rev. Eliab Byram, son of Ebenezer and a graduate of Harvard. John Cary, a master builder, was called from Bridgewater to build the new structure, and worked for the equivalent of 31¢ per day. Rev. John Pierson, a Yale graduate, became pastor in 1753 and was succeeded by Rev. Francis Leppard, a graduate of Princeton, in 1762. It is remarkable that the small community could attract such able and educated men as spiritual leaders.

HISTORY

By the onset of the American Revolution, Mendham was a small but thriving village. There was an established trade route between New York and Hackettstown, a journey of four days. One of the scheduled stops was the Black Horse Tavern, the political, legal and social center of the community, where one could hear all the local news and gossip.

The town was self-sufficient as country towns of that era usually were. Small individual farms provided produce and livestock to answer the needs of each family. Several grist and sawmills were in active operation, taking advantage of the abundant water supply. There were blacksmiths, tanners, cobblers, coopers and other tradesmen, and the centers of Mendham and of Waterville (Brookside) to the east were bustling with activities connected with these occupations.

Nearby was Jockey Hollow, named for the Guerin family, described as high-spirited, brave, liberty loving, French Huguenots who were fox hunters and very fond of the chase. Twice during the American Revolution, Washington chose the Jockey Hollow area for winter encampments of his troops. The surrounding hills provided lookout and signal points as well as some protection for his men. There were several active iron mines and forges within Morris County, which were of great importance to the war effort.

Proximity to Jockey Hollow brought the war close to the lives of the families in Mendham. Inevitably there was some Tory sentiment among the Patriots and this was dealt with summarily, usually by expulsion from the community. Washington's generals were quartered in homes nearby — General "Mad" Anthony Wayne stayed for a brief time in Dr. Blachley's house — and the local people were sometimes called upon to minister to the medical needs of the soldiers. Hilltop Church became a temporary hospital during a smallpox epidemic and a headstone in the cemetery is a poignant reminder of the twenty-seven soldiers who died of this disease. Citizens contributed what they could in the way of food, livestock or even a valuable horse, if necessary, and Washington wrote in a letter that "provisions came with hearty good will from the farmers in Mendham Township". At Washington's request, Lebbeus Dod, son of Stephen, added to his home an armory for the repair and manufacture of muskets.

Other Mendham citizens were strategically involved. David Thompson who earlier had survived a typhoid epidemic in which his parents, five siblings and other close relatives had died within months of each other, was captain of a group of Mendham Minutemen and a member of the Committee of Public Safety. This latter group was established by the Provincial Congress in 1776, to root out Tory dissent and activity. On more than one occasion, George Washington was a guest at the handsome stone house just west of the village center.

Like much of the new nation, Mendham was greatly impoverished at the end of the Revolution, and settled back to being primarily an agricultural community. The mining of iron ore, one of the original attractions to the region, was too expensive to be practical. Many of the local citizens, including some decendants of the original families, joined the westward migration particularly to Pennsylvania and Ohio. The

Dayton family gave their name to Dayton, Ohio.

The devalued currency of the post-war period caused major problems for some citizens of Mendham. John Logan had been appointed commissary to Washington and supplied the army with feed and flour ground in his mill, built about 1770 on the bank of the Raritan in Roxiticus. It is probable that the failure of the new government to reimburse him adequately for expenditures caused his bankruptcy. His property was purchased at a sheriff's sale in 1786 by John Ralston who then operated the mill very successfully until 1829. Records of Ralston's businesses and general store survive, and give a revealing view of the material needs of local residents and the method of barter frequently used for payment. He had a thriving trade with New York and also sent such items as iron and peach brandy by schooner to Augusta, Georgia, receiving molasses, skins and indigo in exchange. In 1826 lime, a component of concrete used to construct the Morris Canal, was ground in this mill. It was quarried on the adjoining farm of Hugh Nesbitt, a business partner of John Ralston. Nesbitt's nephew married Ralston's daughter and their descendants still maintain a home on the property.

The Leddell family purchased the Ralston mill in 1830 and operated it until 1906. It was a hive of activity especially during the 1850's and 1860's when the mines to the north and west in Randolph and Chester Townships were still active. Mule drawn wagons pulled the grain and lime to markets as far away as Newark.

For the early residents of Mendham, it is evident that education was a subject of primary importance. Rev. Henry Axtell, D.D. established the first "Academy" about 1795, approximately on the site of the present Hilltop School. Ezra Fairchild, graduate of Amherst and son of Ebenezer Fairchild of Brookside, conducted a very successful private academy known as the "Hill-Top", situated opposite the First Presbyterian Church. In 1862, William Rankin started a private academy, referred to on the 1868 Beers map as a Classical & English School, in which he compiled a remarkable record. He prepared seventy-six students for college and one hundred fifty as teachers; fifty of his students became clergymen; thirty lawyers; twelve physicians. His school was on Prospect Street, formerly known as Seminary Street. Several other small private academies operated in the village for a time during the 19th century.

Commendable as it was that Mendham produced so many educators and ministers, it was often pointed out that her other major product was the making of whiskey. Liquor was an important cash crop in colonial times because it was in steady demand, non-perishable, and easy and inexpensive to produce. Made from distilled apples, this "apple jack" or "Jersey Lightning" as it was aptly called, was the bane of local ministers who fought unending, unsuccessful battles that were doomed to failure, sometimes for merely practical reasons. The early records of Hilltop Church indicate that twenty-seven of its members had owned distilleries. In the 1820's, a minister of the Presbyterian Church who frequently gave sermons on the evils of alcohol was ungraciously dismissed and told that "nearly all the money that came into Mendham was from the sale of distilled liquor".

Another minor casualty of the apple jack controversy was William Phoenix who was refused a burial plot in Hilltop Cemetery because he kept a bar at his inn. Undaunted, he bought a large plot adjoining the Churchyard and surrounded it with a stone fence. It can still be seen today although as the cemetery has expanded the Phoenix section has been visually incorporated into the whole.

Growth of population was very slow during the 19th century, but some of the local citizens prospered. In addition to John Ralston's successful enterprises, John Marsh had a lucrative business making fine carriages for customers in Georgia, with annual sales reaching $25,000. However, much of this trade ended in 1862 with the onset of the Civil War and his factory stood deteriorating on Main Street until torn down in the early 1900's.

The 1868 map of the Beer's Atlas Company is the first detailed map of Mendham available. It shows a village of eighty-one principal buildings of which sixty-one are still standing. The Business Directory accompanying the Beers map lists a tanner, shoemaker, butcher, blacksmith, cooper and tinsmith, two physicians and a Justice of the Peace. In Brookside, there was a woolen mill, as well as a wagon manufacturer, a miller and other small businesses. The map also lists two boarding houses, both having female proprietors. Many area families took in summer boarders, and old timers recall that families from New York to Philadelphia came to board in Mendham year after year for country air and relaxation.

The most famous of these boarding houses was the Phoenix House. In the 1820's, William Phoenix a former innkeeper at the Black Horse Tavern, converted what had been a young ladies' seminary into an inn. Phoenix ran this inn, in competition with the Black Horse and in trouble with the church, until 1857 when his daughter, Julia, took over. Miss Julia converted the inn and tavern into a genteel boarding house which she ran for fifty years. However, she continued to sell liquor from the outside entrance to the small kitchen she added to the rear of the main parlor. General Abner Doubleday,

credited with the invention of modern baseball, was a frequent guest at the Phoenix House until he built a permanent home nearby, where he died in 1893. Today the Phoenix House is owned by Mendham Borough.

In the last quarter of the 19th century, the major railroads, constructed through nearby towns, did not reach Mendham, perhaps because of the opposition of citizens who did not want such an intrusion into the rural quality of their community. However in the 1880's, because of increasing demand by farmers to the west of Mendham for better access over the hilly terrain to markets near Morristown, the Rockaway Valley Railroad Company was formed. The tracks were laid without a rock ballast bed, and in several places traversed swamp lands. The uneven terrain caused frequent derailments and a rocky ride, for which the railroad quickly earned the nickname "Rockabye Baby". Its principle freight was peaches from Hunterdon County, and during the peak harvesting season passenger cars were frequently sidetracked to allow passage of the perishable crop, making a brief commute a lengthy and uncertain one. The peach blight of 1895 hastened the demise of this local institution and the tracks were dismantled in 1913 and sold as scrap metal during World War I. Remnants of the Rockaway Valley Railroad bed can still be seen near Cold Hill Road and south of Main Street in Brookside.

Another public transportation effort was the establishment, in 1909, of the Mendham Garage Company which ran an auto stage line between Mendham and Morristown. A large passenger car capable of carrying twenty persons traveled between the two towns in 30 to 35 minutes with a one way fare of 40¢ or round trip at 75¢. Friendly competition ensued when Mrs. A. A. Maher, of Ralston, in a frame of mind familiar to today's commuter and car-pooling- mother, felt that she was so frequently on the road with her automobile, she would carry passengers along the same route at the bargain rate of 15¢.

Following the pattern of construction of elaborate country estates in the Morristown area by wealthy families from New York and elsewhere, some large homes were built in Mendham around the turn of the century. Difficult times during World War I, the institution of the income tax, and the effects of the Depression, greatly curtailed this lifestyle. Mendham settled back again as a quiet semi-rural village until a new building boom began in the 1960's and land values, which were listed as $61 per acre in 1881, began to skyrocket.

Today, Mendham Borough and Mendham Township are primarily residential communities. The Black Horse Inn, now a restaurant, receives visitors from near and far as it has for nearly 250 years, and the Phoenix House serves the public as the Borough's town hall. The former village area, now the center of Mendham Borough, has attained Historic District Status from the National Register of Historic Places. It is still the hub of activity in the community, although the former mills and small industries have been replaced by antique shops, real estate offices and banks. Similarly, in Brookside, early homes still line the main street, preserving some of the ambience of a time when small businesses were operated out of these same houses and horses pulled wagons along the unpaved road.

Despite the problems associated with an increasing population, public and private efforts are made to maintain the character and charm of the Mendhams. Concerned citizens have organized, on several occasions to acquire land for the purposes of recreation and conservation, or to forestall industrial or commercial development in favor of a planned and balanced residential growth. The efforts to keep Mendham residential are a recurrent theme in the ongoing history of the town; establishing a kinship with so many of the people who have settled here over two and one half centuries.

Let us let Mendham's architecture tell the rest of the story.

Jeanne Will
Brookside, 1986

Aerial view of Hilltop Church, from the Rotogravure Section of the *New York Times,* January, 1933, ". . . beyond which lies part of the 1,300 acres that will be included in the new Morristown National Historical Park, created by Act of Congress and designed to include the area occupied by Washington and his troops in the winter of 1779-1780." (courtesy of Helen Scholz)

An early view of the Black Horse Inn, from a collection of Inn pictures owned by Anthony Knapp.

Freeman Bros. enterprise, from the papers of Miss Elizabeth Phoenix.

Early post card of Mendham from the collection of Don and Newly Preziosi.

HISTORY

On the road to Mendham,
Bernardsville, N. J.

2313

1

Colonial Times

Early Architecture

The first families to settle the land that became Mendham came from New England early in the 18th century. Although architectural style was not a consideration for those seeking shelter in an undeveloped land, each group of settlers brought a different concept of what form that shelter would take. In New Jersey five distinctive colonial building traditions were used: those of the Dutch, Swedes, Germans, English Quakers and the relocated New Englanders. The folk building crafts and traditions of all these groups can be traced to medieval Europe. Folk building, or vernacular architecture, is the building tradition of the common man expressed in forms developed and passed on over generations, outside the realm of architects, art theory or fashion. Most of Mendham's buildings in all periods are this vernacular architecture.

The early vernacular buildings of Mendham bore no exterior decoration and reflected their utility in a straightforward arrangement of doors and multi-pane windows that were relatively small in relation to wall area. Few could afford paint, so most frame houses and outbuildings in rural 18th-century Mendham were a weathered gray. These were simple functional dwellings surrounded by the fields, sheds and barns necessary to the business of making a living. Architecture as a written system of design ideals and construction principles had not been introduced into the countryside.

EARLY ARCHITECTURE

COLONIAL TIMES

Wooden construction was the building tradition of Mendham's English settlers. For house or barn, they fastened together with wooden pegs a heavy timber frame made of hewn logs. The frame outlined the overall shape and the doors and windows. It was erected on a foundation wall of unshaped field-stones usually laid up without mortar. The all-important chimneys and fireplaces were made of stone, with brick used for finer construction, such as the firebox itself. The frame house was then finished with clapboard on the exterior and lath and plaster on the interior. Sometimes nogging, a varied assortment of soft bricks, small stones, straw, and mud, was packed between interior and exterior walls as insulation.

Such a house required a skilled professional, so carpenters were among the first craftsmen employed in a community. As early as 1742 a deed for land in Mendham was made between "John Lyon of Roxiticus Carpinder" [sic] and Jacob Drake, Black-smith. A carpenter led a team of men in the labor of assembling or raising the frame after he had cut and marked each piece. Careful inspection of rafters in many old houses will reveal the carpenter's inscribed Roman numerals identifying which pieces interconnected.

In Mendham the colonial house was characterized by a broad gable end with a steeply pitched roof, allowing for usable attic space. A broad area of unbroken wall between the top of the first floor windows and the eaves of the roof was also typical. Windows were relatively small due to the high cost of glass and the need to conserve heat in winter.

The most common arrangement of the colonial house in northern New Jersey was a nearly square plan with a door on one side of the facade and two windows. The door opened into a hall which ran to the back of the house and contained a staircase to the upper floor. Two rooms, front and back, opened off the hall. Fireplaces, either angled in the corner to share a common central chimney, or placed in the gable end wall, warmed the two rooms. No fireplace warmed the second floor attic area which was typi-cally used for sleeping and storage. Frequently a smaller kitchen wing was attached with a separate cooking fireplace on the outer wall and a porch across the front for a cool working space in summer. This basic plan was often modified by the original or later owners; yet the form is recognizable enough to have been named the East Jersey cottage by 20th-century scholars because of its dominance in the Province of East Jersey.

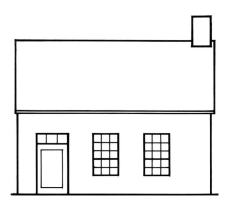

East Jersey Cottage

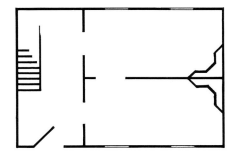

Floor Plan, East Jersey Cottage

Left: Kitched Wing, Blachley House

A classic form of the East Jersey Cottage.

EARLY ARCHITECTURE

Axtell House, Cherry Lane

This restored East Jersey cottage sits
perpendicular to the road, facing to the south.
It is an excellent example of the house style
most commonly built in this area during the 18th century.

COLONIAL TIMES

Keiser House, Brookside

The earliest East Jersey cottages had a high wall between
the first floor windows and roof.
This attic loft area was used for sleeping and storage.
By the turn of the century
these houses were usually built or remodelled
with small windows
to light what had become the second floor bedroom area.

EARLY ARCHITECTURE

Daniel Drake House, Cold Hill Road

This house continues to be occupied by the Drakes, descendants of one of the founding families of Mendham. It faces to the south, not to the road.

Several of the oldest surviving houses in Mendham are East Jersey cottages. The Axtell House is a particularly well-preserved and restored house of this type. The Connet House, another example, was banked into a hillside to gain maximum solar benefit. Siting was critical for the 18th-century builder and, more often than not, a house faced south to catch the sun, with storerooms placed on the cooler north side. Many older houses can be identified because they are not oriented to the road but sit at an angle to it. The Axtell House and the Drake House are two very old East Jersey cottages, both characteristically turned away from the road to take advantage of a southern exposure.

COLONIAL TIMES

Above: Daniel Losey House,
Roxiticus Road

Left: Connet House, Woodland Road

EARLY ARCHITECTURE

Above: Ann Chute House, Brookside

Right: Thomas Knighton House, Brookside

This house was created in 1838 by joining two houses. The original East Jersey cottage is to the right. Moving houses was a common practice in earlier times. An agreement in 1807 between Benjamin Prudden and Daniel Drake permitted Drake "to move, take away, and convert to his own use, a certain dwelling house or tenement which stands adjoining on the west end of the dwelling house where the said Benjamin Prudden now resides". (from the Drake family papers)

COLONIAL TIMES

Elias Babbitt House, Mountain Avenue

The traditional house form of Mendham's early settlers was a low square dwelling, but some larger
two-storied houses were built. This early two-storied house retains the floor plan of the East Jersey cottage.
Note the small size of the windows in relation to the wall surface. The portico
over the front door is a 20-th century addition and is more formal than any other part of the house.

EARLY ARCHITECTURE

Old Presbyterian Parsonage

Moved from its original location, part of this beautifully
restored house may be the oldest surviving
building in Mendham. The right-hand portion
is believed to have been built in 1748
as the parsonage for the Presbyterian church.
The larger portion was added in 1763.

COLONIAL TIMES

Left: Japeth Chedister House, Brookside

A substantial building of early date, the asymetrical facade and absence of detailing mark it a vernacular dwelling. The small attic windows flanking the interior chimney are characteristic of 18th century construction.

Right: James Sheerin House, Tingley Road

The longevity of vernacular house-building traditions is evident by comparing this farmhouse, built in 1911, with the Chedister House, built in 1765.

EARLY ARCHITECTURE

Frederick Pierson House, Brookside

Not all of Mendham's 18th-century dwellings were East Jersey cottages. Another common form was a one-and-a-half story house with a centered front door and small windows flanking it. With one room downstairs and a loft above, this small simple cottage type was often the first home for Mendham settlers. Later, as families grew in size and prosperity, the original house was sometimes merged within a larger, more fashionable dwelling. The Pierson House survives more or less in its original form despite enlargements. A close look at the rear portion or kitchen wing of many larger houses in Mendham will reveal their 18th-century cottage origins.

COLONIAL TIMES

Kitchen Wing, Losey House

The original dwelling, put to a new use when prosperity
allowed for a larger addition.

EARLY ARCHITECTURE

Left: Woodruff House, Main Street

Dormers and a sweeping porch are a 19th-century addition to this early house.

Below: Joseph Sutton House, Corey Lane

Before dormers came into common use in the late 19th century, eyebrow windows were the traditional way of adding light to the second floor.

COLONIAL TIMES

Only a few examples of a house common throughout the American colonies exist in Mendham. This popular English vernacular house is characterized by a five-bay facade, center front door and one-and-a-half-story height. The Woodfruff House is a good example, although it now includes a porch and dormers added in the Victorian era. The Tingley House combines the center entry cottage with another familiar New England building form, the saltbox. Characterized by a long rear roof sloping directly from the second floor to enclose a first floor addition, the saltbox is uncommon in Mendham, where additions were typically built at the sides rather than onto the back.

Tingley House, Tingley Road

This saltbox shape is unusual in New Jersey, but the wide space below the roofline is typical of this area, and sets it apart from the New England form.

EARLY ARCHITECTURE

COLONIAL TIMES

Because Mendham lies along the western boundary of what used to be East Jersey, a few structures are more typical of the old West Jersey cultural region, which extended to the Delaware River. Many German settlers arriving in William Penn's colony traveled up the river and spread out along its banks. The German influence in colonial architecture is most noticeable as a building tradition in stone. Fieldstone was used for the walls of houses and barns, chimneys, foundations and fences. As one travels west from Mendham the incidence of stone buildings increases until, across the Delaware River in Pennsylvania, stone is the norm for colonial buildings. One early stone building is the Cooper House, a dwelling clearly related to Delaware Valley tradition. Its tall narrow shape and central front door are building characteristics more common to southeastern Pennsylvania then to northern New Jersey.

Above: Nesbitt Barn

Stucco was frequently applied over rough stone walls to insure a watertight building.

Left: Cooper House, Stone House Road

EARLY ARCHITECTURE

Right: Brodshaw House

An early stone house built up-river
about a quarter of a mile
from the Logan mill.

Far Right: Jonathan Logan Mill, Ralston

This old stone mill is close to the river,
its source of power.
The massive stone walls
were built to withstand flood, fire,
and the jarring of heavy millstones
and wooden gears.
Although it is now a residence,
the origins of the building are
apparent in its design and location.

The fieldstone mill at Roxiticus, now Ralston, was built in 1747. Stones were laid up just as they came from the ground, without being shaped and faced. Openings for doors and windows on the ground floor were arched, and oversized stones were used to stabilize the corners of the house. The stonework was carefully executed, although is does not bear comparison with skilled European masonry of the same period. Because the construction of a stone building required extra effort and time, it was probably chosen for the Logan Mill, as it was for other mill buildings, to guard against fire. Milling created flying sparks from the millstones, and piles of grain were likely candidates for spontaneous combustion.

The stonework of the Brodshaw House is less refined than that of the Logan Mill. Window openings were simply bridged by large flat stones. Sometimes rough masonry like this was covered with stucco. The great strength of the walls is suggested by the depth of the doorway.

COLONIAL TIMES

EARLY ARCHITECTURE

Georgian

By the mid-18th century, American colonial building had been influenced by English Georgian architecture. The presence of settled communities and a general degree of prosperity enabled construction of larger buildings with more detailing. American Georgian architecture, named for its correspondence with the reign of the English monarchs, George I, II and III, was a colonial translation of high-style English architecture, which was based on the work of the great Italian Renaissance architect Andrea Palladio. Palladian architecture looked to symmetry and harmony of proportion as the basis for good design and to the classical world of ancient Rome for details.

Imposing size and the formal arrangement of facade and interior characterize both American and English Georgian architecture. The Georgian style, with its ancient Roman and Italian motifs, was more decorative than earlier colonial building. Even the simplest Georgian house had a pediment or entablature over the centered front door and classical designs on the fireplace mantels.

In a colonial house, cooking, eating, child care, spinning, and sleeping might have all taken place in the same room. The larger Georgian house with its prominent center hall gave independent access to rooms designed for specific uses and afforded a privacy theretofore unknown.

The Georgian style was adopted by the wealthy throughout the colonies. Regional variations exist, but they are fewer and less noticeable than the distinctive regional and national characteristics of vernacular 18th-century houses. No matter what the cultural background and tradition of an area, Georgian architecture was selected by the American gentry of the 18th century.

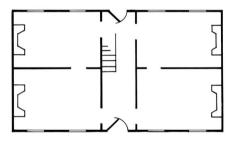

Georgian Floor Plan

GEORGIAN

COLONIAL TIMES

In time, elements of the Georgian style were incorporated into vernacular buildings. The versatility of the Georgian center hall plan made it a favorite by the end of the 18th century and its popularity continued well into the 19th century. Although colonial-period Georgian houses were built chiefly by the well-to-do, after the Revolution, elements of the style were widely adopted. A vernacular house built by a craftsman-builder of the early 19th century was more likely to be a derivative of the 18th century Georgian style than of the earlier regional types.

Today only two 18th-century Georgian houses survive in Mendham. The Blachley House shows the symmetry of the Georgian style and a centered front door embellished with a classically-inspired entablature and moldings. Unlike English prototypes, the service wings are not symmetrical, but extend from only one side of the house. This asymmetrical plan is a typical example of a traditional building pattern carried over into a more formal house.

Above: Ebenezer Blachley House,
Corey Lane

This reconstructed Georgian house was originally built by Dr. Blachley, who helped found the New Jersey Medical Society and later served in the Revolutionary War.

FarLeft: Roff House,
Washington Valley Road

Georgian symmetry and pedimented doorway grace this simple colonial farmhouse.

GEORGIAN

Right: William Rankin House,
Prospect Street

This house, built in the 1860's,
a century after the first Georgian
buildings, illustrates the enduring
popularity of the style.
It was the home of Dr. Rankin
who ran the last of Mendham's
renowned academies in an adjacent
building, now demolished.

Far Right: David Thompson House,
Main Street

Built in the 1770's to face south,
this handsome house sits
with its back to the road.
Mr. Thompson, a member of one of
Mendham's earliest families,
commanded a company of militia during
the Revolutionary War.

The Thompson House of 1774, an example of the adaptation of the Georgian style to the use of local building materials, was built of fieldstone and then stuccoed. During the Georgian era it was a frequent practice to enhance an ordinary material or surface with a fancier veneer. The wooden facade of George Washington's house at Mt. Vernon was carved and then coated with paint containing sand, to make it look like masonry. Many fancy Georgian houses had false windows put in place to insure a balanced exterior.

The Georgian influence on vernacular architecture lingered across New Jersey into the 19th century. A number of these later Mendham examples, like the Rankin House, have the central hall plan, symmetrical facade and prominent entrance of the 18th century style.

COLONIAL TIMES

GEORGIAN

Federal

Federal-period architecture, like the Georgian style which preceded it, was based on classical forms. The Federal style corresponded to the Federal period in America, 1780 to 1820. It was associated with European architecture of the period, but many consider it to be the first American architecture. Although newly independent, Americans continued to look abroad, particularly to England, for the latest in fashion and the arts. Details of Federal architecture reflected increased knowledge about ancient Roman buildings as the science of archaeology developed in Europe.

Exteriors of Federal style buildings became flatter and plainer, while interiors generally became more ornate. Windows were larger both in size of individual panes of glass and in overall dimensions. Curves occurred more frequently than in earlier Palladian-inspired work. Round or elliptical shapes appeared as fanlights over doors, archways and even in oval or circular rooms. Elegance, lightness and restraint characterized the best Federal style buildings. This represented not so much a break with the more vigorous Georgian classical tradition as a refinement of it.

In Mendham the Federal period was a time of increasing prosperity, based on greater contact with the larger world. A growing population caused Chester Township to separate from Mendham in 1799, and in 1805 Randolph Township was established. In 1806 the Washington Turnpike, now Rt. 24, was begun, linking Morristown with the Delaware River at Easton, Pennsylvania and creating larger markets for local farmers. The turnpike brought travelers through Mendham, filling the old Black Horse Inn and contributing to the general economy.

FEDERAL

Phoenix House, Main Street

Built soon after the completion of the
Washington Turnpike in 1806,
the Phoenix House accommodated
travelers and summer lodgers
for over a hundred years.
Given to the Borough in 1938,
it has recently been refurbished
to house administrative offices,
and public gatherings.

About 1820, a building, which became a hostelry known as
the Phoenix House, was built across the road from the Black
Horse Inn at the crossroads in the center of town. A fine local
interpretation of the Federal style, its wide gambrel roof is typical
of many New Jersey and New York buildings of the period. The
four large end-chimneys, each pair joined by a low parapet wall,
are characteristic of Federal architecture. Although obscured by a
large portico added in 1838, the Phoenix House itself is simply
detailed. The fanlight above the front door is the only explicit
Federal-style ornament. Inside, the mantels were elaborately decorated, featuring the elliptical gouge-carved patterns
characteristic of Federal design in northern New Jersey.

The Phoenix House is the oldest brick building in Mendham.
Brickmaking was established at an early date in the American

COLONIAL TIMES

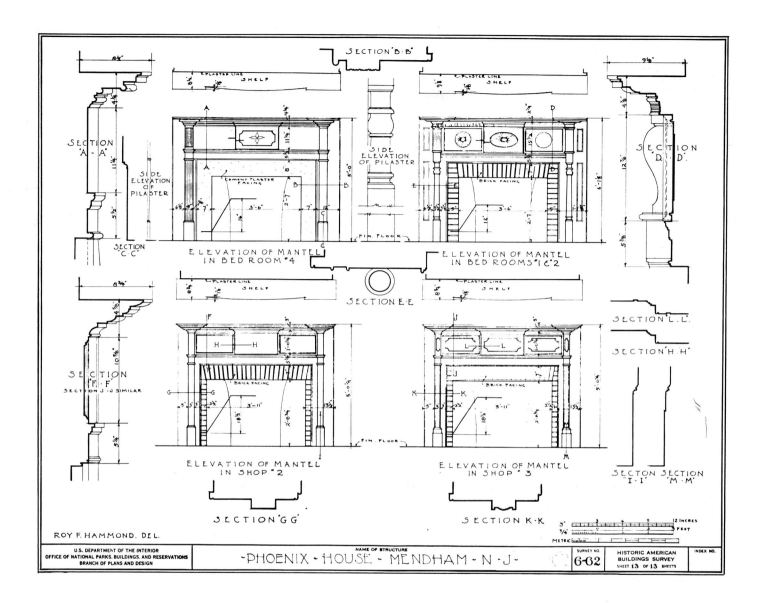

SECTION 'B·B'

ROY F. HAMMOND, DEL.

ELEVATION OF MANTEL IN BED ROOM #4

ELEVATION OF MANTEL IN BED ROOMS #1 & 2

SECTION E·E

ELEVATION OF MANTEL IN SHOP #2

SECTION 'G·G'

ELEVATION OF MANTEL IN SHOP #3

SECTION K·K

| U.S. DEPARTMENT OF THE INTERIOR OFFICE OF NATIONAL PARKS, BUILDINGS, AND RESERVATIONS BRANCH OF PLANS AND DESIGN | NAME OF STRUCTURE ·PHOENIX·HOUSE·MENDHAM·N·J· | SURVEY NO. 6-62 | HISTORIC AMERICAN BUILDINGS SURVEY SHEET 13 OF 13 SHEETS | INDEX NO. |

colonies: by 1610 in Jamestown, Virginia, and 1629 in Salem, Massachusetts, with bricks mixed, shaped and fired by hand. Not until 1792 was the first patent for a brick-making machine granted. Bricks were heavy and cumbersome to transport, so brickyards and brick buildings were generally located near each other. The source for the bricks used in the Phoenix House is not documented but they might have come from nearby Chester Township. The 1853 map of Morris County identified a brick yard just to the west of Mendham and south of the Washington Turnpike. Judging by the few brick structures built in the area, the output of this brickyard must have been limited.

HABS, Library of Congress

Detail from Phoenix House interior.

FEDERAL

Above: Hilltop Manse, Hilltop Road

Right: Cary House, Mountainside Road

All of Mendham's early brick buildings were painted to weatherproof the soft porous brick.

Brick was also used for the parsonage of the Hilltop Church when it was erected in 1832 and for the nearly identical Cary House. Like the Phoenix House, the Hilltop Manse and the Cary House have gambrel roofs and fanlights over their front doors. Although later in date than the nationally-defined Federal period, these houses were very much in the Federal style, indicating the longevity of familiar architectural forms in rural areas like Mendham.

COLONIAL TIMES

FEDERAL

William Leddell House,
Tempe Wick Road

The Leddells were an important
Mendham family, respected and prolific
over many generations.
Legend has it that the stones
used to build this fine house
were gathered from the campsites
of General Washington's Army,
which spent the winters of 1779
and 1780 just north and east of this
property at what is now
Morristown National Historic Park.

Several large houses constructed in Mendham during this period attest to the growing prosperity of the community and its developing industries. In Roxiticus, now Ralston, a cotton mill began operating in the early 1800's, and its owner built a handsome Federal house nearby. The Ralston Manor was built on a center-hall plan. Tall brick chimneys punctuate each side of the gambrel roof, and the first floor fireplaces are visible on the exterior as brick insets in the clapboard wall. This was the practice for late 18th and early 19th-century New Jersey buildings, perhaps to avoid the potential hazard of dried clapboads over the hot fireback.

The dam on the Passaic River that created Leddell Pond was the site of a saw mill in the 19th century. By mid-century a grist mill was also operating there. Both of these activities must have been profitable, for the Leddell family lived next door in a large fieldstone Federal-style house. Its gambrel roof and side-hall plan were typical of Federal buildings in the region, although the use of stone and the pedimented doorway were more common to the Georgian style.

COLONIAL TIMES

Ralston Manor, Ralston

The gambrel roof, double end-chimneys and
large window openings are regional characteristics
of the Federal style,
popular from the 1790's to the 1820's.
The two-over-two sash windows,
and slate roof are later 19th century additions.

FEDERAL

Above: Jacob Thompson House, Main Street

This house was built to face the Washington Turnpike, laid out in 1804. Its gambrel roof, paired chimneys, and elliptical fan and sidelights surrounding the front door are typical Federal features. The first floor windows are late-19th-century replacements.

COLONIAL TIMES

Left: St. Mark's Parish, Main Street

In this house changing architectural taste can be read
in the multiple additions and details.
The gambrel-roof Federal portion
substantially enlarged an early 18th-century cottage,
now the rear kitchen wing, again enlarged in the
mid 19th century with the flat-roofed section to the right.
These disparate elements are unified
by the bracketed cornice and matching portico.

Above: Aaron Losey House, Brookside

In size and plan this house is typical of the colonial period,
but the gambrel roof, paired end-chimneys and transom
over the front door are
all hallmarks of the Federal style.

FEDERAL

Hilltop Church, Hilltop Road

Moved from a rise
just above the river to the west,
a Presbyterian church
has overlooked the town
from this site
since 1745.

One of the most formal of all Mendham's Federal buildings was not built in the Federal period but at the time of the Civil War. This anachronism is the Hilltop Church, built in 1860. The present Hilltop Church is the fourth church building on the site since its founding in 1745, a site which was the unfortunate target for lightning twice in the 19th century.

This style of church architecture, which is most closely identified with Federal-period New England, actually had its origins in 17th century England. Christopher Wren, charged with rebuilding London after the Great Fire of 1666, created a simple church form accented by a tall steeple. A dramatic break with Gothic churches, Wren's neoclassical model was widely imitated in colonial American cities with the help of English builders' books. After the Revolution the Wren formula reached smaller towns and inland villages. During the Federal period an explosion of church-building occurred as communities prospered and outgrew their frame meetinghouses of colonial days. In 1816, when Mendham replaced the old meetinghouse on the hill, it would most likely have been in this style. Thus the Hilltop Church that was built in the Federal period became the model for future reconstructions. Notable Federal characteristics of the 1860 building include the large multi-pane windows and the thin elegant lines of the steeple.

Some elements of the 1860 Hilltop church were not Federal, such as the Gothic window frames on the facade. These fanciful details were part of a new view of architecture that had come into vogue during the middle of the 19th century, adding romantic touches to Mendham's vernacular buildings and inspiring masterbuilders to produce new building forms.

COLONIAL TIMES

FEDERAL

2
Years of Prosperity

The Romantic Revivals that changed Mendham's appearance during the 19th century were another series of architectural styles inspired by past cultures. A focus on the picturesque was common to the arts at this time. In architecture it was accompanied by major improvements in building materials and techniques. New technology made building a cheaper, less labor-intensive craft. Products like cut nails, smoother and larger panes of glass, machine-sawn laths and machine-made door panels appeared between 1800 and 1840 and were adopted enthusiastically throughout the country.

The surviving account books of John Ballentine, a Mendham store owner of the 1820's and 1830's, document the sale of building materials. Darius Babbitt purchased "2 hundred oak shingles" in 1822, probably as siding for a building. Nails were also sold at the general store. In 1839 Ballentine sold to Charles Thompson fish oil, lamp black, linseed oil, Venetian red, white lead, yellow ochre and turpentine, all components of house paint. That same summer a man bought tobacco and a "palm hat", another purchased "coarse shoes [for] self and a pair of fine shoes for Elizabeth".

The ability to purchase building supplies and luxuries even in a small village reflected the improved commerce of the countryside. People in Mendham were in touch with the fashions and ideas of the larger world. Their increasing sophistication is apparent in the many romantically-fashioned early 19th century buildings that survive today.

Greek Revival

The fascination for classical architecture in the Georgian and Federal eras continued into the 19th century with a new emphasis on ancient Greek forms. In place of the arches, ovals and smooth-surfaced exterior walls of the Federal period, architects and builders focused on horizontal and vertical lines and the bold simple detailing of the ancient Greek temple. The style that developed became known as Greek Revival.

Educated men knew the classics and most people were familiar with ancient mythology. Allusions to the classical world in art, literature or architecture were widely understood. The story is told that in 1852 the Reverend Dr. Hastings, pastor-elect of the Mendham Presbyterian Church, was astonished by the level of education of Mendham's citizens. He noted that even the farmers quoted Latin and Greek.

Benjamin Henry Latrobe, an English architect, is credited with America's first Greek Revival building, erected in Philadelphia in 1798. There was a lengthy time lag between urban and rural acceptance of an architectural style in 19th-century America, but popular interest in the symbolism of Greece soared after 1821, with the news of the Greek War for Independence. Architects and builders took advantage of this political and social attention by producing a number of guides that showed how to adapt ancient Greek architecture for American use.

The most popular American builders' guides to feature the Greek Revival were by Minard Lafever. Lafever, who was born in neighboring Morristown, had established himself as a carpenter in Newark by 1824. Lafever was not a common name in the area

Drawing from *The Modern Builders Guide*, M. Lafever, (1830).

There are no doorways in Mendham with columns and paired doors, but the outer door enframement is evident in many local Greek Revival buildings.

GREEK REVIVAL

Greek Details

While most of the elaborate Greek designs in builders' books were not used in Mendham, the rosettes featured in the drawing below, from *The Modern Builders Guide*, were incorporated in this doorway.

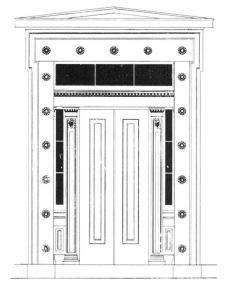

and he was quite likely related to the Lafever family living in Mendham during the 19th century. In 1833 Lafever published *The Modern Builders Guide,* one of the most widely used sources of American Greek Revival designs. All Lafever's books demonstrated his familiarity with both sophisticated architectural design and the instructional needs of the American craftsman.

These builders' guides modified designs and plans that were originally meant for execution in masonry to allow for wooden construction. They contained some exterior drawings of buildings but were dominated by patterns for details, rules of proportion, and practical advice to the carpenter, such as how to attach a capital to a column, or figure the quantity of wood needed for a particular staircase. With the help of such handbooks, local builders learned to combine traditional house forms with popular classical elements.

Local carpenters also adapted the designs to suit their tools and skills, compensating for a lack of historic authenticity with inventiveness, boldness and solid workmanship. Their use of the classical elements of architecture transformed many humble dwellings to genuinely accomplished buildings. The result in most instances was a new and vital American architecture.

Discussion of Greek Revival in Mendham must include the work of masterbuilder Aaron Hudson who was born in Mendham in 1801 and died there in 1888. Hudson practiced his craft from the 1830's to the 1870's and described his occupation as Carpenter-Builder for the 1850 Census. The details of his life are unknown; from whom he received his training and what his sources were remain a mystery.

Aaron Hudson's first commission in Mendham is said to have been the portico of the Phoenix House in 1838. The bold double-height piers, a signature of Hudson's, were a prominent part of

his most distinguished buildings. The use of square piers rather than classical columns was a frequent recourse of the country carpenter; they were easier to construct and their effect was similar.

The porch of the Phoenix House all but obscures the delicate Federal-period building behind it. The strong verticals of the piers and the bold horizontals of the wide plain entablature emphasize the structure of the porch. Together they suggest a more massive building than actually exists. Elements like the piers were not merely decorative, but an important visual support for the heavy entablatures, and a practical support for the extended roof.

Phoenix House Portico

GREEK REVIVAL

THE MODERN BUILDERS GUIDE.

BY M.LAFEVER.

.Gallier des for Lafever   W.S.Barnard sc

Drawing from *The Modern Builders Guide*, M. Lafever, (1830)

No records survive to identify Aaron Hudson's buildings, but folklore attaches his name to some, and many others may be attributed to him on the basis of stylistic similarities. Certainly there can be no doubt that he designed the house where he lived during the height of his career. It was built about 1840 and appears to be derived from the frontispiece design in Lafever's *Modern Builders Guide*. Hudson's house is dominated by a projecting pediment supported by double-height piers like those of the Phoenix House. Since the temples of ancient Greece were the wellspring of the entire revival style, the pediment was used on all manner of American buildings, although Hudson's house is the only surviving example in Mendham. The center of the facade and the gables are flushboarded instead of clapboarded, a technique found repeatedly in Mendham's wooden Greek Revival buildings, to suggest the smoothness of dressed stone.

YEARS OF PROSPERITY

Aaron Hudson House, Hilltop Road

Hudson was a Mendham carpenter who designed and built many local buildings in the Greek Revival style. He must have used Lafever's drawing as inspiration for his own house, constructed in 1840 on the site of an earlier dwelling.

GREEK REVIVAL

Nicholas House, New Street

A flushboarded facade distinguishes the 1842 Leddell House. This house and its twin, the Nicholas House, undoubtedly came from the same hand, perhaps Husdon's. Both are essays in geometry and proportion, square shapes capped by shallow pyramidal roofs. Applied pilasters support entablatures punctuated by tiny windows and in each case a raised basement acts as a podium to further dignify the small house.

YEARS OF PROSPERITY

The nearly perfect classical facades of the Nicholas and Leddell houses mask one of the major drawbacks of the Greek Revival style: the need to arrange the interior space within a geometrically rigid plan. The Leddell House was designed with a wide hall occupying the full length of the house, allowing an elegant over-sized entry but only two rooms on the principal floor. The Nicholas House may have been built somewhat later, for its plan was altered to allow for more rooms at the expense of a smaller and less grand staircase. Both houses sacrifice convenience for beauty, particularly in the bedrooms. Located behind the entablature, they are lit only dimly by eyebrow windows and have low sloping ceilings, due to the pitch of the roof.

Dr. William Leddell House,
Roxiticus Road

GREEK REVIVAL

It was a common practice for the owner and his builder to choose traditional house forms and merely dress them in Greek Revival details, or any of the other fashionable revival styles of the period. The two-and-a-half-story side-hall house, popular in New Jersey in the Federal period, served well as the base for Greek Revivl embellishments. The Homan farmhouse is flushboarded across the facade and sides, including the earlier left wing. Cornerboards with simple capitals, a porch with pier supports, and simply framed windows impart great dignity.

The DeMunn House is similar in form to the Homan House. Its prominent corner pilasters, an encircling porch with wide entablature and pier supports are all typical of rural Greek Revival houses. Although no viewer will mistake a flushboarded wall for masonry, an emphatic contrast exists between the flushboarded Homan House and the clapboarded DeMunn House. The clapboard's strong horizontal lines diminish the visual impact

Joel Homan House,
Mountainside Road

of the cornerboards and the sense of weight and solidity, making
this house more vernacular and less Greek.

In many ways the Greek Revival style marked the transition
from Georgian and Federal classicism to the more fanciful styles
that followed. The later Romantic Revivals used more exotic
architectural forms from different cultures and periods.

DeMunn House, Main Street

GREEK REVIVAL

Left: Calvin Willet House, Roxiticus Road

Throughout the Greek Revival period the vernacular East Jersey cottage was used as the base for Greek detailing. The wide space between the first floor and the roof line was often punctuated with eyebrow or knee-high windows, to help define the area as an enlarged Greek frieze.

Below: Nesbitt House, Ralston

Originally a small dwelling that faced to the south, the Nesbitt farmhouse was substantially enlarged in the mid 19th century. The vernacular Georgian-type house was dressed with a Greek Revival double-height portico similar to the one added to the Phoenix House. The brick cladding is a relatively recent addition.

YEARS OF PROSPERITY

Above: Ballentine House

The pilasters and flushboarded
facade mark this as a
Greek Revival building.

Right: L. Losey House,
Roxiticus Road

The heavy piers of the front porch
are stylistically related to a
Greek colonnade and create
an imposing entrance
for an otherwise simple house.

GREEK REVIVAL

Gothic Revival

Gothic Revival was another of the romantic approaches to architecture of the early 19th century. While the classical lines of Greek design followed ancient rules of proportion that called for reason and order, Gothic design featured asymmetry and appealed to one's emotions.

Although the two styles are very different, they were both popular throughout the early 19th century. Like Greek Revival, Gothic Revival had its roots in 18th-century England. The first Gothic building in America was erected in 1799, only one year after the first Greek Revival building. The two styles were frequently combined, particularly in rural areas.

The first hint of Gothic in Mendham is found in Aaron Hudson's 1838 renovation of the Phoenix House, where Greek inspired piers frame a Gothic-arched railing for the second-floor porch. In Hudson's own Greek Revival house the central second floor window is a Gothic-style pointed arch with diamond-patterned panes, imitative of medieval leaded glass. The Gothic-arched windows in the facade of Hilltop Church are the only clue to its mid-19th-century date, for otherwise its styling reflects the classicism of previous generations.

The hallmark of Gothic Revival architecture is the pointed or Gothic arch. Other elements include batten siding, spires and turrets, all of which emphasize verticality. The Gothic emphasis on irregularity and asymmetry in both plan and elevation allowed for greater freedom of room arrangement than did classical symmetry. In conservative Mendham few buildings followed an irregular plan, and the Gothic style was limited to a decorative applique on traditional house forms.

By far the largest body of original Gothic architecture survives in the great cathedrals and churches of Europe. In America Gothic Revival was used for houses, schools and commercial buildings, but its most frequent use was for churches. This is also true in Mendham where the only complete Gothic Revival style buildings are the churches of St. Joseph and St. Mark.

Gothic Revival Window,
Hilltop Church

GOTHIC REVIVAL

St. Joseph's Church, Main Street

Despite modern siding and some alterations, the basic form remains intact.

St. Joseph's Roman Catholic Church was constructed between 1859 and 1860. Its design and execution is credited to Aaron Hudson. Although Hudson's classically styled Presbyterian Church was rising concurrently, he chose an authentic Gothic style for St. Joseph's, perhaps because of the association of Gothic with Catholicism and the great European cathedrals.

St. Joseph's is an example of Carpenter Gothic, the name given to the style when it is adapted to wood. Pointed-arch openings were used to contain both doors and stained glass windows, and the vertical thrust of the steeply pitched roof culminates in a small peaked steeple. The wooden buttresses have no structural purpose in this small frame building and serve only as a stylistic element. Gothic Revival design promoted decorative richness and

YEARS OF PROSPERITY

color both inside and out. St. Joseph's stained glass windows and decorated walls are important features, but only fragments of the original interior painted decoration survive.

Gothic Revival was popular for a long time. In Mendham thirty-four years separate its first and last appearance. The principal structure of St. Mark's Church was built in 1872-73 for the new Episcopal congregation. The choice of Gothic design for Episcopal churches became nearly universal in the 19th century

St. Mark's Church, Main Street

GOTHIC REVIVAL

after the English Ecclesiological Movement declared the Gothic church the only suitable structure for Christian worship. At St. Mark's, Gothic verticality is emphasized by the lines of the board-and-batten siding. The church is actually quite small, but the enormous roof and well-proportioned lancet windows give it the presence of a larger building.

St. Mark's is said to be copied from Richard Upjohn's Grace Episcopal Church in Jersey City, now demolished. Upjohn and his son Richard Jr. were outstanding and prolific American church architects active in the 1840's and 1850's. Their books included designs to be built for modest sums of money and inspired the construction of hundreds of Gothic Revival churches across the country. If not actually modeled after an original Upjohn church, St. Mark's is similar to several published Upjohn designs.

Gothic Revival was favored by 19th-century-America's most popular patternbook author, Andrew Jackson Downing, landscape architect, house designer and self-styled tastemaker. Downing brought architectural romanticism to the middle class and, in the process, firmly fixed in the American consciousness the idea of a single-family suburban house.

Downing's books differed from those of Minard Lafever and earlier writers. They contained little building information, but featured engravings of different house exteriors surrounded by trees and gardens. Unlike earlier architectural renderings where buildings existed in a void, Downing's drawings promoted landscaping as an integral design feature. His text included advice on color, interior decoration, furniture selection and types of shrubbery, all selected and designed to carry out the theme evoked by the particular style of the house.

One of the houses in Mendham indebted to Downing is the original Methodist Parsonage, which was built about 1850 and follows his precepts in the use of board and batten siding, casement windows and a bay window. An exact patternbook prototype has not been identified, but the parsonage is certainly similar to cottage examples illustrated by Downing in his 1850 book, *The Architecture of Country Houses.*

Scholars identify several distinct phases of Gothic Revival, to distinguish Gothic-style churches and colleges built well into the 20th century. Mendham's Gothic architecture exhibits a rural vitality and naivete missing in later manifestations of the style.

DESIGN XVI
BRACKETED FARM HOUSE OF WOOD

Drawing from *The Architecture of Country Houses*, A. J. Dowing, (1850).

Old Methodist Parsonage, Main Street

The house is one version of the many cottages designed and published
by A. J. Downing. He wrote, "What we mean by a cottage,
in this country, is a dwelling of small size, intended for the
occupation of a family, either wholly managing the household cares itself,
or . . . with the assistance of one or two servants." Downing
went on to state that simplicity was the dominant character of cottages,
but "domestic enjoyment could be enhanced by addition of a porch or bay window."

GOTHIC REVIVAL

Italianate

The third of the great Romantic Revivals was called Tuscan or Lombard and today is known as the Italianate style. It was inspired by the 17th and 18th-century villas of northern Italy, a favorite country of the educated 19th-century traveler. Since Italian influence on music, art and poetry was widespread, it is not surprising that this popularity extended to architecture. The adaptation of Italy's relatively contemporary architecture, itself a vernacular version of classical Roman architecture, was the freest by far of the Romantic Revivals.

No matter how appealing, villas for the warm Italian climate were not practical in most of America. Instead, individual elements including brackets, arches, columns, pediments, balustrades and quions were combined and recombined on traditional house forms. The style was immensely popular, and its ubiquitous presence on commercial buildings, houses, churches and schools led some contemporary observers to conclude that it would become the sole national style of American architecture.

ITALIANATE

Main Street

The tree lined vistas along Main Street in Mendham Village show a lasting influence of the 19th century landscape movement.

The unity of Italian villas and their gardens also influenced the growing landscape movement in America. Frederick Law Olmsted's Central Park in New York City is the greatest achievement of this movement. The beauty of this park influenced villages and towns everywhere, which led to planting trees in town squares and along roads, and a new approach to landscaping around houses.

The principal features of the Italianate style in America were bracketed eaves and round-arched windows. Just as the pedimented Greek temple was reduced to a projecting portico on some Greek Revival buildings, the pediments of Roman architecture were reinterpreted in Italianate buildings over windows and doorways and as front-facing gables.

YEARS OF PROSPERITY

A gabled facade, pedimented windows and bracketed eaves embellish the large Cole House, which can also be described as a mid-19th-century villa. A villa was a house located neither in the center of town nor isolated in the country. It was surrounded by gardens and trees, but was not a farmhouse, and its architecture evoked a picturesque image. The curved driveway in front of the house was another feature associated with landscape architecture, and was an esthetic improvement over the straight rutted cart track most common in the 19th century.

Other houses in Mendham display features similar to the Cole House but they cannot be considered villas because they occupy smaller in-town lots. One example is the Second Presbyterian Parsonage built in 1863. The church, demolished in 1900,

ITALIANATE

stood across the street and was also Italianate in style. The parsonage is dominated by a facade gable and in it the round-arched window so charactersitic of the style. Like so much Romantic Revival ornament in Mendham, these details were merely grafted onto a traditional center-hall house.

High-style Italianate houses were rarely symmetrical and never had flat facades. Instead they were punctuated with corner towers, central projections, bay windows and boldly three-dimensional moldings. The irregular "T" plan of the Henry Drake House is more characteristic, and displays some of the best Italianate detailing in Mendham. Its original porch is gone but other elements survive, such as the closely bracketed eaves combined with a dentil molding, pedimented window frames and paneled chimneys.

YEARS OF PROSPERITY

Henry Drake House,
Cold Hill Road

ITALIANATE

Left: Marsh House, Main Street

Below: Stubenrauch House,
Washington Valley Road

YEARS OF PROSPERITY

Like the Second Presbyterian Parsonage, the Marsh House is a traditional house with Italianate details. Again there is a facade gable with round-arched windows lighting the attic. The patterned slate roof is original, one of only a few Mendham survivors of a common 19th-century roofing material. Scroll brackets under the eaves continue up into the gables, and the ornamental porch, which once extended across the facade, is Gothic Revival, a reminder that few buildings were stylistically pure.

The same facade gable of the Cole House, Parsonage and Marsh House can be seen on simple farmhouses like the Stubenrauch House, where it is the only reference to architectural fashion in an otherwise timeless vernacular building. With its traditional plan and lack of ornament, it could have been built anytime in the 19th century.

The flat roof was another feature brought directly from Italy and made more practical in non-Mediterranean climates with the invention in 1852 of bituminous roofing. Mendham's only flat-roofed Italianate structure was originally built as a shoe shop in the 1870's in the center of the village of Brookside.

The Italianate style, like the Gothic Revival, lasted beyond the Civil War but became heavier and more baroque in character. The simplicity of Italianate architecture in Mendham reflected both rural conservatism and the lack of wealth needed to build more extravagantly.

ITALIANATE

3

The Work Place

Mills and Factories

Industry was an integral part of America's 18th and 19th-century communities, and Mendham was no exception. Its many streams provided power for grist mills and sawmills, while wagon factories, harness makers, butchers and carpenters supported the agricultural industry. The tannery, blacksmith's forge and cooper's shop were sources of noise, dirt, smells and activity that would be quite out of place in today's suburbia. Although Mendham never developed into an industrial center, mills and factories appeared and disappeared until the early 20th century.

One of the earliest factories was a textile mill located along the stream near Ralston. The first meetings which led to the formation of the Methodist Church were held there in 1800. In 1819 a Morristown newspaper, the *Palladium of Liberty*, carried advertisements for the sale of a mill for fulling and dyeing wool on Water Street (Brookside) operated by John and Abraham Byram. That same year the *Palladium* reported that one Thomas Knighton operated a sawmill and turning mill near the Byrams' factory. Knighton also set up an unsuccessful glass factory in the same area.

MILLS AND FACTORIES

These 19th century industries were housed in wooden sheds and outbuildings which were easily removed when they had served their purpose. The coach factory located on Main Street in Mendham stood empty for over fifty years until 1912, when its demolition was hailed as a great civic improvement. The site of a former blacksmith's shop is still serving today's transportation needs as a modern automobile dealer and gas station. However, about all that remains of Mendham's industrial past are the dams and bits of foundation wall such as those found at Leddell Falls and Smith's Gristmill site.

It is surprising that a 1853 map identifies only one distillery, since other documentation suggests that a large trade in liquor, mainly apple jack or "Jersey Lightning", flourished in the community. In 1855, the Rev. Cox noted of his Hilltop congregation, "I had, if I remember right, from 18 to 20 distilleries under my pastoral care, and I found them very impracticable and untoward parishioners . . ." (Calvin Davis memoirs).

Charles Thompson's account books for his general store refer to the frequent use of spirits and cider as a medium of exchange. One example is the March 6, 1824 transaction by Abram Hudson, who traded one barrel of cider, bundles of straw, and leather for cash and a sheep. Another customer traded eleven gallons of spirits for various items.

Not all the liquor was used for trade. In 1813, Daniel Drake received a summons from the church leaders:

"You are hereby required to attend the Academy on Thursday the 14th Inst., at 4 o'clock pm to testify before the Session what you know in support of a charge of intemperate drinking and using prophane [sic] language, instituted against Mr. Abner Leach."

Throughout the 19th century, Mendham clergy fought intemperance, but one Presbyterian minister preached too often about the evils of alcohol and the making of strong drink. The Rev. Hay was dismissed in the 1820's after only eighteen months at his post, being informed that "nearly all the money that came into Mendham came from the sale of distilled liquer [sic]."

The old Nesbitt Mill that became the Laughlin Distillery in the early 1900's is the single Mendham cider mill or commercial distillery still intact. Abandoned for many years, this large unadorned stone building is now being restored.

THE WORK PLACE

John Nesbitt Mill, Ralston

Built as a grist mill, this large stone structure became
a cider mill and distillery about 1908 when it was purchased
by the Laughlin family, who also operated a distillery on Hilltop Road.
Mendham's distilleries were closed by the Volstead Act of 1919
and the Federal enforcement of prohibition.
Although the building has been empty for many years, in 1985
work was begun to restore the mill to its former appearance.

MILLS AND FACTORIES

Left: Site of Smith's Mill, Brookside

Built by James Smith between 1745 and 1750, this mill was one of the first enterprises to operate in the Brookside area.

Below: Site of the Rockaway Valley Railroad

The Rockaway Valley Railroad, known affectionately as the Rockabye Railroad, was built through Mendham in 1888. The tracks were laid well north of the village center and the railroad did not have much of an economic impact on the area. Most of the old right-of-way has been preserved as park land. It acts as a buffer between burgeoning suburban developments and as the Mendham's portion of Patriots Path, the Morris County intercommunity walking path.

THE WORK PLACE

Small industries and mills diminished in importance during the 19th century as the Industrial Revolution introduced the large factory with its increased productivity. Mendham did not keep pace with the nation's move to large-scale operations, perhaps because of a lack of raw materials and poor transportation connections. No canal served the area. The many streams were fine for water power but too small for navigation, and the most important 19th-century innovation in transportation, the railroad, arrived late and had little economic impact on the community.

The Rockaway Valley Railroad, known locally as the Rockabye Baby, was built from Whitehouse to Morristown in 1888, primarily for shipping produce, mainly peaches, to eastern markets. It ran through Brookside, skirting the villages of Mendham and Ralston. The two rudimentary wooden stations were demolished and the tracks torn up in the 1920's.

Mendham's lapse into rural somnolence during the latter part of the 19th century was reflected in a loss of population and greatly diminished building activity.

Iron Truss Bridge,
North Branch Raritan River

The most common American bridge built between 1850 and 1925 was the metal truss bridge, a design utilizing many small pieces to create the long span needed to cross a stream. There are two basic types, the Pratt and the Warren, each named for their inventor, although hundreds of variations were developed. These bridges were prefabricated by specialized bridge companies and erected throughout the country in rural and urban settings. This is a Warren truss, identified by the triangular outline of the supports. It is a simple, functional design, still used by present-day bridge engineers.

MILLS AND FACTORIES

THE WORK PLACE

Left: Leddell Falls, Tempe Wick Road

Above: Site of the Leddell Mill

MILLS AND FACTORIES

Barns

When Mendham's principal business was farming, barns of all sizes were built throughout the community. Although the remains of barns and farm outbuildings are more numerous than mills or the sheds of other industries, much has been lost from the agricultural landscape.

Traditional American barns fall into two characteristic types, the English barn and the Pennsylvania-German barn. Although named for geographic points of origin, both were widely known by the early 19th century, and construction of one or another type was a farmer's preference, not necessarily a clue to his cultural background. English barns were built on one level, usually on a three-part plan consisting of a center threshing floor that could be driven through, flanked by stock aisles. Pennsylvania or bank barns were built into a hill or embankment. They had a ramp and a wagon entrance on the uphill side and animal bays across the exposed lower level. Both types were built in Mendham. Heavy timber construction, like that used in framing the earliest houses, was used for barns long after more modern techniques revolutionized house building. Many barns incorporated portions of earlier structures. Close examination of a frame may reveal peg holes or notches which have no use in the present structure, but are evidence of previous use in another building. Establishing construction dates for barns is difficult because identical methods and materials were used over a long period of time.

Banked Barn

English Barn

BARNS

Below: English Barn

Left: Banked Barn

Far Right: Two 20th-century Barns

THE WORK PLACE

BARNS

Outbuildings

Above is a stone stable from the Cromwell Estate,
left is the smokehouse of the Drake Homestead,
right are a silo and corn crib from the
Franklin Farm Estate,
and far right is a converted corn crib.

THE WORK PLACE

BARNS

Above: Shingled Cupola

Left: Spring House

Below: Barnyard

THE WORK PLACE

After the Civil War, the trend toward more tools and larger farm machinery created the need for larger barns. The Victorian era also introduced the barn cupola which increased ventilation and light, and became an ornamental feature similar to the gables and towers of the new residential buildings.

By the 20th century, Mendham's small hilly farms were no longer competitive, so innovations in barn design, involving new materials like concrete and galvanized iron, were not used. Farming had all but disappeared in Mendham and the barns that remained were used for other purposes or gradually allowed to decay.

The barns that were built in Mendham between 1890 and 1930 belonged to the new estates. Beautifully designed, often in a style to complement the main house, they were meant for display as well as use, and were not burdened with the need for economic self-sufficiency.

Above: Shingle Style Estate Barn

Below: Weathervane

BARNS

Stores

Commerce expanded and became more specialized in America's larger cities during the 19th century, but in Mendham, and hundreds of small towns like it, the general store and the small shop prevailed. Directories of the 19th century identify some of Mendham's commercial activities. The Brookside Business Directory for 1868 listed:

E. M. Byram, Wagon Manufacturer

S. L. Byram, Blacksmith

M. M. Connet, Miller

S. E. Conner & Son, Farmers & Millers

A. Losey, Postmaster & Dealer in Boots & Shoes

Jonathan Lilly, Woolen Manufacturer.

The Mendham Business Directory for the same year included:

Wm. Babbitt, Leather Manufacturer

Calvin Day, Dealer in Stock

Geo. W. DeGroot, Butcher

Wm. H. Meslar, Manufacturer of Copper, Tin,
    Sheet Iron Ware & Dealer in stoves

Theo. W. Phoenix, Merchant

The listing also included a pastor, doctor, teachers, and boarding-house proprietors.

STORES

The General Store, Ralston

This store was in operation before 1786. Restored by the Ralston Historical Society and opened to the public as a museum in 1964, it is the oldest building still standing in the United States to have housed a Post Office.

The Ralston General Store is Mendham's oldest commercial building. When it closed in 1900 it enjoyed the distinction of being the longest-lived post office in the country. In size and material it resembles typical residential buildings of the first half of the 19th century, but the facade arrangement identifies it as a place of commerce, with an overhang for shelter where patrons could gather and talk. Account books dating back to the 1840's indicate that this was truly a general store, with merchandise including soap, nails, stamps and candy.

THE WORK PLACE

The present Brookside Post Office occupies another old business site. As early as 1868, and probably long before then, this corner in the center of the village was occupied by a store and post office. With its gable-end to the street and a center front door flanked by large display windows, this store represents the most common vernacular form for early 19th-century commercial buildings. Generally, windows projected as bays or the door was recessed, to give prominence to the windows and their merchandise. A 19th-century shoemaker's shop, now a residence, features the characteristic gable-end facade and large display windows of the former shop. The double front doors further identify its commercial origin.

Although building materials and proportions were the same, there were differences between early commercial and residential structures. The differences widened in the 20th century, with the increased size of commercial buildings and their use of new or unusual materials. Plate glass was developed for storefronts around 1890, and remained almost exclusively a feature of commercial building until the 1950's fashion for picture windows in houses.

Above Right:
Shoe Shop, Mountain Avenue

The commercial origins of this building are clear in the gable-end facade, extra large windows for the display of merchandise and double front doors. It was used as a shop by Henry Drake in the early 1800's and by David Carlisle, a shoemaker, in the 1880's. It was converted to a residence in the 1960's.

Above Left: Brookside Post Office

STORES

Above Left: Old Firehouse, Main Street

The old firehouse is the symbol of Mendham Borough's incorporation. Defense against fire was the principal reason for the creation of a local water company that necessitated the separation of the more densely populated village from the outlying farms.

Above Right:
McNulty Store, Hilltop Road

Built in 1905, this commercial building became Mendham's Post Office after the borough was incorporated in 1906. The Plate glass show windows were a new technological improvement over the smaller panes used in the 19th century.

The commercial buildings constructed in the early 1900's were the largest structures on Main Street. The three-story firehouse, built in 1905, contained storage space for fire-fighting equipment, apartments, and a large social hall on the upper floor that was used for dances, school graduations and occasionally as a movie theater. The firehouse was noteworthy not only for its size, but for the fact that it was built with a new material, concrete block. Decorative blocks like these, with one face molded to imitate rough-cut stone, were manufactured in Bayonne, New Jersey, and were popular at the turn of the century.

The same rusticated blocks were used on the first floor of the McNulty Store, also built in 1905. This storefront is typical of the period, with its recessed center door between two large display windows. Although built as a grocery, it was the Mendham post office for over seventy years.

During the first half of the 20th century, improved roads and the automobile enticed people to the more prosperous commercial areas of Morristown, Dover and Bernardsville. As a result, no new commercial buildings were added to Mendham's business center until the 1960's, when suburban expansion prompted the construction of a shopping center at the eastern end of town.

THE WORK PLACE

Right: Freeman Brothers, Main Street

Charles and Frank Freeman operated several businesses at this location at the turn of the century. The first floor was used as a dry goods store and bakery, with a printing shop in the rear. Next door, the brothers operated a blacksmith and carriage shop that evolved into an automobile service station by the 1920's. It is reputed that windows from the old Second Presbyterian Church, demolished in 1901, were used when this store was constructed in 1902.

Below: The general use if the automobile has resulted in the suburban shopping center where stores enclose a large parking area. A grocery store usually anchors the center surrounded by a variety of specialty shops that cater to the day-to-day needs of the community.

STORES

4

The Victorian Era

Mendham did not participate in America's post-Civil War rush toward industrialization and urbanization. Lack of rail service and the small scale of local industry left the community an economic backwater. The population declined slightly from 1860 to 1890 as people left the village to find opportunity elsewhere.

Some of the best evidence for Mendham's economic stagnation is the scarcity of Victorian architecture. Unlike the vigorous building activity of the first fifty years, construction during the last half of the century was scant. Buildings that did appear were generally modest and less influenced by architectural style then in earlier years.

The art and craft of building sustained profound change in the late 1800s as the result of mechanization and new technology. Standardization of the size of lumber, nails, window sash, and roof shingles, as well as floorplans, made building both cheaper and more efficient. The development of balloon framing, a predecessor of today's light wooden building frame, streamlined construction. Gone were the days of the master carpenter hand-notching and pegging together a building frame. Factories produced doors, windows, shutters, and the hallmark of the age, jigsawn wooden ornament known as gingerbread. All these could be purchased directly from a manufacturer's catalog or at local hardware and building supply stores. Jigsawn ornament, found most frequently on Victorian-era front porches, was mass-produced in a huge variety of patterns. Separate elements were combined by owner or builder to confer a degree of individuality on buildings that might otherwise be identical.

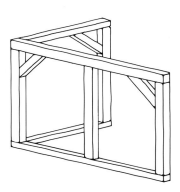

Post and Beam Construction

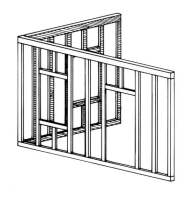

Balloon Construction

THE VICTORIAN ERA

The term Victorian, when applied to American architecture, denotes a time period roughly corresponding to the English Queen's reign (1837-1901), and not to a particular style. Within that time a number of styles developed that were characterized by an abundance of decorative detail, irregular massing and polychromatic exteriors.

As with the earlier Romantic Revival styles, architects were inspired by historic designs and motifs. But rather than recreate old forms, they selected fragments from ancient buildings and recombined them. Innovative materials and structural parts were hidden by ornamentation that tried to recall earlier hand craftsmanship. Favorite elements of the Victorian-era builder included chimneys borrowed from Tudor England, towers from Norman castles, windows from Gothic churches or 17th-century cottages, and exterior cladding of stone, brick, clapboard, or shingles, sometimes all on the same building.

Patternbooks proliferated, but unlike earlier 19th-century builders' books, their audience was the middle-class consumer, not the builder or tradesman. Patternbooks pictured house elevations and plans, with page after page of decorative novelty. Plans sometimes showed large closets, central heating and interior bathrooms. These were new concepts in home comfort, although many houses built before 1900 lacked one or more of these amenities. In 1863 Henry Hudson Holly, a popular patternbook author, observed about one of his designs, "Over this pantry, in the second story, a bathroom might be made; but none is here introduced on account of the expense."

Because Mendham did not participate in the expansion and growth of the late 1800's, only a few houses were built during this time. In contrast, nearby Morristown, which experienced a surge of prosperity, was the scene for the construction of scores of houses in all the fashionable architectural styles of the late 1800's.

One of the earliest of the post-Civil War Victorian styles was the Second Empire, an imitation of French architecture during the reign of Napoleon III (1852-1870). Its hallmark was the mansard roof, with steep sloping sides and ornamental curbing or cresting. No Second Empire houses were built in Mendham, but two earlier dwellings were remodelled with mansard roofs. These houses displayed an awareness of urban fashion, but they lack the complex, three dimensional massing and decoration associated with the best examples of the style.

THE VICTORIAN ERA

Above: Charles Morris House, Brookside

Builders in the Victorian era were free to combine elements from different styles. The stonework on this house is a feature most commonly associated with the 18th century, while the plan and proportions are Federal. The columns at the doorway are Gothic Revival, the brackets under the cornice are Italianate, and all are capped by the French-inspired mansard roof.

Right: Caroline Bartow House, Mountain Avenue

This was one of the many houses in Mendham that accommodated summer boarders in the late 18 and early 1900's. Alterations to a traditional side-entrance house created a spacious dining room in the bay window addition, and small bedrooms on the third floor, behind the mansard roof.

THE VICTORIAN ERA

Somerhurst, Mountainside Road

Joseph Somers built this estate house as a summer retreat in 1888. The date is carved in a plaque over the pedimented entry to the front porch.

Mendham's most ambitious Victorian structure is the Somers House, built in 1888. This large house is an example of the Queen Anne style, characterized by a symmetry, irregular massing of forms, especially of the roofline, and a liberal mix of materials. The stone first floor and shingled second floor, corner tower, purposely mismatched dormers, and projecting gables are typically Queen Anne. The disparate parts are tied together by the wide porch that wraps around the tower, across the facade, and extends out over the driveway to form a covered carriage entrance or porte cochere.

Other examples of the Queen Anne style in Mendham were more subdued. A large elaborately trimmed porch and a mix of clapboard and shingle siding were the most commonly used local adaptations.

THE VICTORIAN ERA

Above: Thomas Lowery House,
Talmadge Road

The Lowery farm, overlooking
Mendham Village from the south, was
prosperous enough to enable the
family to build a large farmhouse in the
Queen Anne style in 1892. This house
was destroyed by fire in 1983, but has
since been carefully reconstructed to its
original design.

Right: John Hoffman House,
Main Street

Galvanized metal shingles were new in
the Victorian era. They were an
inexpensive roofing material and their
patterned effect was an important
component of the Queen Anne style.

THE VICTORIAN ERA

Right: George DeGroot House, Prospect Street

Below: Robert Babbitt House, Mountain Avenue.

THE VICTORIAN ERA

Above: Petty House, Main Street

Right: Quimby House,
Hardscrabble Road

The variety of Victorian jigsawn
ornament is evident on these pages. On
the vernacular house, in conservative
Mendham, it was usually confined to
the porch, but at the Quimby House it
also appears as a lacy bargeboard
on the eaves.

As in the past in Mendham, traditional vernacular house
forms served as a base for the application of fashionable trim.
During the Victorian era this was generally concentrated on the
facade, particularly the new front porch, or verandah. Houses
with surviving porches illustrate the variety of ornament available
at that time. Lathe-turned and square spindles were typically part
of porch railings, and shaped shingles on the gables formed
patterns to contrast with clapboard siding. Galvanized metal roofs
added further texture, set off by bargeboard, or jigsawn gingerbread at the eaves. In recent years, much of this important
architectural detail has been removed or covered with modern
siding.

THE VICTORIAN ERA

Left: Coe House, Main Street

The two 19th century multi-family houses that survive today were both built across the street from industrial enterprises, a coach and carriage factory on Main Street and a woolen mill in Brookside.

Below: Double House, Brookside

Multiple-family dwellings are rare in Mendham, as they ara a building type more associated with large factories and the urban streetscape. Nevertheless, several did exist and, like this one built in the early 20th century, they continued the vernacular building traditions of the early 19th century.

THE VICTORIAN ERA

Above: Christopher House, New Street

Left: Schenk House, Main Street

According to the 1850 census, the majority of the people of Mendham village listed their occupation as "Laborer". In 1905, 467 of the 992 working residents of Mendham labeled themselves as "unskilled laborers" and 138 as "skilled". Non-farm workers lived in small frame cottages throughout the village. These two relatively untouched examples retain the small size and simple detailing of the typical 19th-century "working man's" dwelling.

The few small Victorian houses that survive in Mendham seem tiny for the large families typical of the time. The cottage now known as the Christopher House was built as a laborer's house in the vernacular tradition. Its narrower gable, centrally placed chimney and extended eaves distinguish it from colonial buildings. The extensively renovated Schenk House is another small dwelling enriched by a front porch with jigsawn trim.

Families unable to afford their own houses often rented part of a multiple-family dwelling. Mendham's two double houses which survive from that era were built with the traditional side-hall plan. A longer late-Victorian rowhouse of five side-by-side units on Main Street was demolished in 1975.

THE VICTORIAN ERA

Right: Palmer House, New Street

Below: Illustration, American Architecture, Palliser, (1878)

Despite the fact that relatively few laborers and craftsmen moved to Mendham during the Victorian era, some 19th-century urban-type houses were built in the village. The planbook house, so-called because its form was standardized in so many late-19th-century patternbooks, is characterized by a side-hall, a roof turned so that the gable faced the street and a front porch. This house, with its long narrow proportions, was perfectly suited to the development of single family housing on small urban lots. Streets lined with these houses are found in almost every city and town east of the Mississippi.

Although the new building and up-dating of older houses that took place in Mendham during the late 19th-century was relatively modest in comparison, it related in spirit to the grand Victorian housing being built in the surrounding more prosperous communities.

THE VICTORIAN ERA

Below: Illustration, American Architecture, Palliser, (1878)

Right: Samuel Wychoff House, Main Street

Below Left: Emma Bochoven House, Mountain Avenue

Below Right: D. Sutton House, Main Street

THE VICTORIAN ERA

5

Age of Comfort

Shingle Style

The United States became a world power by the end of the 19th century and Americans began to reject thoughts of artistic and cultural inferiority. In all of the arts there was a new appreciation of American themes, and for the first time, cultural influences began to flow toward Europe as well as from it. In architecture there was a need to develop an American style, free from the ornamental allusions to ancient civilizations which had always characterized high-style building.

In the search for indigenous themes, architects looked to early American colonial buildings, both formal and vernacular. Two apparently divergent styles developed, the Colonial Revival and the Shingle Style. The Shingle Style sprang from the vernacular buildings of colonial New England, while Colonial Revival was based on a reinterpretation of that area's finest Georgian buildings. The Shingle Style was allied to the Arts and Crafts Movement, which advocated a return to nature and a simpler life. It was a forerunner of modern architecture in the expression of the building materials' basic characteristics, the reduction of applied ornament and the informality of plan. Colonial Revival was more formal, more decorative and ultimately more popular and long-lasting as colonial-style buildings continue to be constructed today.

Although both approaches disdained the machined ornament and fanciful details popular in the late 19th century, neither rejected the many technological innovations developed in the Victorian era. Plumbing and electricity became standard in

SHINGLE STYLE

Mendham Methodist Church, Main Street

This is the second building to house the Methodist congregation, formed in 1827. When completed in 1893 it was certainly the most architecturally fashionable building in Mendham. In 1899, the Rev. W.B. Judd wrote, "It is a beautiful church of modern style of architecture, built of a native gray stone, the mason work being of an especially handsome character. The interior finish is of oak, giving the rooms a light and cheerful appearance . . . The building is heated by furnaces, and lighted with gas, manufactured by a machine in the basement. In structure, appointments, and attractiveness, the church is a gem and may well be a source of pride to the people. It is valued at $15,000."

AGE OF COMFORT

domestic interiors, kitchens were designed with stoves rather than fireplaces, and cupboards and closets were built-in features of even the most modest dwellings. The more important Colonial Revival and Shingle Style houses were designed by architects, but eventually, plans and drawings of both styles were available in pattern books and magazines.

By the end of the century the Morristown-Mendham-Bernardsville area was a fashionable locale for the affluent. Colonial Revival, Shingle and the later Eclectic Revival styles, first appeared in Mendham in the large estates built on the hills to the north and south of the village. These architect-designed estates were dominated by enormous houses complemented by outbuildings, including garden follies, gate houses, stables and barns, all designed to match the style of the big house.

The Shingle Style took its form and name from the American tradition of building in wood. It has a complex architectural pedigree with antecedents in English Victorian architecture, the writings of the American architectural theorist A. J. Downing, the English art critic William Morris, leader of the Arts and Crafts Movement, and the rediscovery of colonial America's vernacular buildings. The creators of the style, intent on developing a new American architecture, blended these many influences. The Shingle Style was used primarily for domestic architecture; and in Mendham, the only public building to incorporate the style was the new Methodist Church, completed in 1893.

The key element of the style is its shingled cladding. Wooden shingles covered wall and roof to create a seamless surface. Shingle Style buildings had an organic quality not found in earlier Victorian designs, and an appearance of age, because of their rambling asymmetrical forms and minimal stylistic detail.

A comfortable and informal interior arrangement often featured a live-in hall with a large turning staircase. Warm earth tones, exposed wood, and airy window treatment replaced the dark formal drawing rooms, carved woodwork and heavy drapes of the Victorian era. Interior walls were opened with wide doorways so that rooms flow into one another. As a result, interior room arrangement is not obvious from the exterior and window placement appear random. These windows are larger and often banded or grouped. They were also often placed around the front door which is rarely front and center. The Shingle Style building

SHINGLE STYLE

Dean Sage Estate, Bernardsville Road

The rambling Sage house illustrates several of the multi-national influences which inspired the Shingle Style. The post-and-beam construction of the entry suggests Japanese wooden temples and the sweeping roof eaves have a Far Eastern flavor. The formal symmetrical arrangement of the facade is derived from Georgian or classical models, and the eyebrow windows and multi-pane window sash intentionally recall English cottages.

is dominated by its roof, which shelters one or two floors of living space marked by dormers and gables, and porches recessed within the roof line rather than extending as a separate element.

The wooden shingles are frequently complemented by porches and chimneys of cobblestone or fieldstone. The body of the house was not painted but stained a natural tint or left to weather, resulting in gradations of color which blend the building into the landscape and help to achieve a timeless look.

In Mendham several smaller houses were built as an offshoot of the style. Their design also emphasized materials in their natural state, with unpainted shingles and rough uncoursed stone. The efficient informal layout of this smaller middle-class house was both a design consideration and a recognition of the declining use of domestic servants.

The original effect of many surviving Shingle Style buildings has been lost by the replacement of weathered or stained wooden shingles with asphalt on the roof and paint on the walls. This contrast in materials and color visually separates wall and roof, where a blur between the two was intended.

AGE OF COMFORT

Right: Ernest Garabrant House, Main Street

When this house was constructed in 1902 the building which housed the Babbitt School, in operation from 1881 to 1901, became the kitchen wing. Although synthetic clapboard replaces the original shingles, the house may still be identified as a Shingle Style building by its complex massing, steep roof and multiple window types.

Below: Elliscourt

This hilltop estate, built for Frederic Cromwell in the late 1880's, is now used by the Sisters of Charity. The rambling asymmetrical house is an excellent example of the Shingle Style.

SHINGLE STYLE

Craftsman

In the early years of the 20th century, many of the ideas about simplicity in design, the natural expression of materials, and an appreciation of hand-crafted objects, came together in *The Craftsman*, a magazine published by Gustav Stickley. Stickley began his career making furniture, but his interests were broader than home furnishings. He founded *The Craftsman* to express his ideas about utility and simplicity, and to feature houses he believed were appropriate to a modern way of life. *The Craftsman* featured small houses which were economical to build and easy to maintain. These so-called Craftsman houses are the architectural and philosophical descendants of the Shingle Style, although they were created for a mass market and are rarely seen in larger, architect-designed versions. Stickley's magazine did not embrace a particular style, but rather an attitude about housing that was expressed in a variety of building types.

Craftsman cottages all share a horizontal emphasis and minimal decoration. Other identifying features include grouped windows set in plain frames, often with the upper sash divided into multiple panes over a single lower sash, eaves extended well beyond the wall line, and exposed rafter ends. Clay tiles, slate, or wooden shingles were laid to produce a rough or shaggy effect on the roof. The support piers for broad porches are massive and squatty and rest on cobblestone or rusticated concrete bases. Surface texture was important on Craftsman houses, created from rough natural materials or man-made materials such as concrete.

These houses were popular in Mendham village at the turn of the century. Many were stuccoed and display the first non-wood

CRAFTSMAN

Thayer House, Orchard Street

The horizontal ground-hugging lines of the bungalow is markedly different from the verticality of 19th century styles. Even the dormer window of this typical bungalow, built in 1927, has a long low appearance, quite different from the Victorian dormer.

exteriors since the handful of brick buildings erected during the Federal period. The houses were easy to build using plans and specifications available from *The Craftsman* or similar publications. If no builder was available, a house of this type could be ordered by mail. From 1908 to 1939, Sears Roebuck sold prefabricated houses including Craftsman inspired designs. Other manufacturers sold them as well, in ready-to-assemble kits, complete to the kitchen sink.

One of the most popular variations of the Craftsman house was the bungalow. It was classically a one-story house with a low-pitched roof and surrounding porch tucked under the extended eaves, but larger bungalows with steeper roofs and dormers created space for a usable second story.

AGE OF COMFORT

Right: Albert Taylor House,
Main Street

Originally, the term bungalow was applied to one-story houses, but it soon came to include two-story variations like this one. The front dormer is an unusual combination of a single shed roof and separate windows. Here, the characteristic bungalow porch is enclosed with banded windows.

Below: Talmage Bungalow,
Talmage Road

The hipped roof of this bungalow forms a deep front porch within the body of the house. Note the extended roofline and exposed rafter ends at the eaves, both typical features of the style.

CRAFTSMAN

Another popular two-story Craftsman house was large and
square and topped by a pyramidal roof. This easy to recognize
house-type was not given a name. Modern architectural historians
have dubbed it the American four-square, a descriptive if not very
poetic title. The house itself is more practical than poetic, but its
simple lines, generous rooms, and largely care-free exterior made
it "the most house for the least money", as proclaimed by the
advertising of the day. The plain exterior allow the materials and
their texture to be shown to full advantage.

The popular acceptance of Craftsman houses spread quickly
across the country in the early 1900's. Many New Jersey towns
were transformed from village to suburb during this period, and
bungalows and other Craftsman houses filled street after street. It
was at this time, 1906, that Mendham Borough was created within
Mendham Township. Neither community was subject to a suburban development boom but the Craftsman houses that were built
were in Mendham Borough, the former village area, along Main
Street and Mountain Avenue, and Orchard Street, the only new
street developed during those years.

AGE OF COMFORT

Above: A. Seeley Hutchinson House, Prospect Street

Stucco and concrete were not new materials in the early 20th century, but they were the subject of much interest and experimentation. Several designers, including Thomas Edison, built concrete houses as examples of modern, inexpensive shelter. Although concrete as a material for domestic architecture never became as popular as its promoters hoped, it was in common use between 1910 and 1930. These two Craftsman houses were constructed of stucco on a hollow tile core about 1915.

Right: John Tiger House, Prospect Street

CRAFTSMAN

Colonial Revival

The Centennial Celebration of 1876 inspired a revival of early American arts, furniture, and architecture. Taking advantage of this interest, American architects combined Victorian-era expansiveness with design elements of New England's most elegant colonial houses to create the Colonial Revival style. This style first became popular in the 1890's, and in various forms, has remained so ever since.

Detailing for the Colonial Revival style was nearly always overscaled, as if it needed to be emphasized to be recognized. Pedimented doorways or entry porticoes, heavy cornices, and extra embellishments such as balustrades, giant columns, and fanlights were popular. Dormers were used extensively, although this Victorian-era feature was uncommon in the 18th century. The enthusiasm for daylight within the house, introduced in the Shingle Style, resulted in large windows and bigger panes of glass which could not have been produced in earlier times.

One of Mendham's fanciest Colonial Revival houses, the De-Groot House, is a good example of how classic colonial motifs were mixed together and given new uses. The typical Colonial Revival house displayed enough of these modern hallmarks to be easily distinguished from 18th century originals. However, a few careful replications were constructed which are difficult to differentiate from the original. In Mendham several vernacular Georgian farmhouses were remodelled with Colonial Revival details to achieve a grandeur that would not have been seen in this small community until the end of the 19th century.

Colonial Revival Doorways

Doorways in the Colonial Revival style include multiple elements and more elaborate detail than the original Georgian designs.

COLONIAL REVIVAL

Left: Windymere, Talmage Road

Extensive alterations and additions in the 1920's transformed a vernacular farmhouse into a spacious Colonial Revival house. The arched portico at the front door and the bell-roofed wellhouse are features more elaborate than would have been built in colonial Mendham.

Below: Franklin Farm, State Highway 24

This stone Colonial Revival house was built for former New Jersey Governor Franklin Murphy in 1910 - 1914. Its architect, H. Van Beuren McGonegal, created a number of monuments in the Classical Revival style. McGonegal designed the park buildings for the Essex County Park Commission, where he worked with the Olmsted brothers, who also landscaped Franklin Farm.

AGE OF COMFORT

Right: Robert McKean Thomas House

When the old Pitney farmhouse burned to the ground in 1918, Mr. Thomas, Sr. moved the old hay barn onto the original foundation to create this gracious Colonial Revival house. The kitchen wing to the right was fashioned from a little old house which was also one of the original farm buildings.

Below: Elliscourt Farm, Hilltop Road

When the 19th century McMurtry farm became part of the Cromwell family estate it was named Elliscourt Farm. The house was enlarged and remodelled in the Colonial Revival style. The original three-bay side hall house, described in chapter one, is the right hand portion.

COLONIAL REVIVAL

Left: Dr. George DeGroot House, Prospect Street

Dr. DeGroot established his medical practice in Mendham in 1906. This large Colonial Revival style house, which he had constructed in 1912, stands in marked contrast to the simple frame houses around it. The grandly scaled classical detailing includes the only Ionic columns in Mendham.

Below: Reginold Robinson House, Prospect Street

This 1935 house is based on a design published in *Architectural Forum* from a competition for small, well designed houses. Note the differences between this Tidewater colonial copy and the colonial-era architecture of New Jersey: Brick exterior walls, the centrally placed door, peaked dormers and slate roof are materials, fashions and technologies that did not exist in 18th-century Mendham.

AGE OF COMFORT

Mendham Free Public Library,
Hilltop Road

While red brick with white painted trim or light colored limestone accents was often used for Colonial Revival buildings, none were constructed in Mendham until the Mendham Free Public Library was built in 1935. This is a representative example of the style executed in these materials and is similar to countless public buildings constructed across America throughout the early 20th century.

The demand for architecture based on American colonial themes continued through World War II and the housing boom that followed. It is the single most popular style today. All of the housing tracts built in the Mendhams since the early 1960's, when the building boom reached this area, have incorporated the colonial-style design elements of multi-pane windows, shutters, and a Georgian or Federal type doorway.

Mendham Free Public Library,
Hilltop Road

Mendham's first library was a collection of religious books, made available for borrowing in 1797 by the Mendham Library Company. The present-day organization began in 1911 and was housed in St. Mark's Parish House. In 1931, Mrs. Louise Forsythe Demarest bequeathed the land and funds for a new library building. When opened in 1932, this Colonial Revival structure was known as the Sarah Forsythe Demarest Memorial Library, in honor of the donor's daughter. An addition, which doubled the size and matched the original structure, was added in 1976 through the generosity of former mayor Andrew Fletcher.

COLONIAL REVIVAL

Eclectic Revival

The romanticism of the 1800's did not vanish with the new century, but did diminish in architectural importance. Fantasy buildings, recreated Norman castles or Tudor cottages, Spanish villas or French chateaus, were a trend contemporary with the practical Craftsman house and the decorative Colonial Revival style. These European revivals include such a number of inspirational sources that they are considered together in architectural history as the Eclectic Revival style.

The Eclectic Revivals were lavish with authentic detail and modern comforts. The same careful study of early American buildings that influenced the Colonial Revival style was applied to historic European models, and architects were careful to keep these new buildings authentic to a particular time and place. As with the Colonial Revival buildings, few of the Eclectic Revivals were actually replicas of existing buildings, but rather new creations, influenced in massing and detail by the old.

The first and finest examples of Eclectic Revival style buildings in Mendham appeared in the grand estates of the turn of the century. Old English or Tudor Revival was a popular local choice, perhaps because of its connotation of old family, old money and a genteel life. Great effort was made to create the illusion of age in new buildings of this style, including purposefully staining the masonry, constructing sags and dips into the roof, and the use of small mullioned windows. Landscaping was also important to help achieve the appearance of age in a new building. In a 1929 magazine article on the newly-constructed estate now known as Three Fields, the landscape architect and his model for the grounds received as much coverage as the buildings.

As with the Shingle and Colonial Revival styles, smaller versions of Eclectic Revival buildings were eventually constructed. Though never as popular as the Colonial Revival, a number of Eclectic Revival cottage-style dwellings were built in Mendham.

ECLECTIC REVIVAL

Groendyke House and Store, Main Street

When this unusual building was constructed in 1909 it was the first time brick had been used in Mendham since the Federal period. This modern brick is very different from that used on earlier buildings; it is hard and dark, and laid to demonstrate the mason's skill. The corbeled parapet of the corner tower and stepped gable over the store suggest a medieval castle.

AGE OF COMFORT

Right: Anthony Cacchio House, Orchard Street

Below: Radke House, Mountainside Road

Modest versions of Eclectic Revival style houses were built from the 1930's to the 1950's. In the best examples, the picturesque image is the result of richly colored and textured materials, attention to the detail around windows and doorways, and a multi-dimensional facade.

ECLECTIC REVIVAL

AGE OF COMFORT

Above: Glenowre, Mountainside Road

Glenowre was built in 1908 for Daniel and Sarah Moran in the Tudor style, one of many now referred to as Eclectic Revival. Moran was a civil engineer who specialized in designing the foundations for tall and difficult-to-construct structures. Highlights of his long career include the Woolworth Building, which was the tallest building in the world when completed in 1912, and foundations for the George Washington Bridge in 1932, and the San Francisco-Oakland Bay Bridge, in 1935.

Far left: St. John the Baptist Cemetery Gate

An Episcopal convent is a perfect setting for this 20th century Gothic style cemetery gate. American Gothic Revival was at its height of popularity in the 1840's and 1850's, but elements of Gothic architecture were used through the 1930's, particularly in ecclesiastical and university buildings.

ECLECTIC REVIVAL

Three Fields, Cherry Lane

This country house was built in 1929 for Benjamin Mosser by the architect Greville Rickard. When completed, the estate was featured in the magazine *Architecture,* where it was described as being "in the French style." The bulk of the house is broken into small units with the additive quality of a farmhouse that has grown over generations. Steep tiled roof and casement windows lend a European flavor. The whitewashed brickwork and the stable roof with built-in bumps and sags are also meant to convey a look of age and permanence.

AGE OF COMFORT

dos Passos Estate, Tempe Wick Road

Dr. dos Passos greatly admires the great chateaus of
France, and worked closely with his architect,
Campbell Voorhees, to create this sumptuous Eclectic
Revival house in 1931.

ECLECTIC REVIVAL

6

Modern Mendham

Today Mendham's built environment reflects many of the attitudes and traditions begun in the early 20th century, particularly in the continued parallelism of a clean-lined modern architecture and a decorative historical architecture. As in the 19th century, there remains a split between high-style architecture and vernacular building; indeed, at no other time in the past has the division between the two been so noticeable. Modernism, high-style architecture without historical detailing, has been chosen by only a few for architect-designed, custom-built houses. Subdivision houses on small or large lots represent today's vernacular architecture. In Mendham these houses reflect a continuing preference for "colonial" detailing, although their construction techniques and materials are thoroughly modern.

MODERN MENDHAM

Sade House

A residence carefully designed and sited to take advantage of the sun's warmth and light, the Sade's house was created by architect Harry Russell III in 1975.

In Mendham, the detached, single-family house centered on a relatively large lot, has been favored since the first builder's subdivision, Country Lane, was begun in 1960. Local zoning encourages this type of development. More intensive residential development with surrounding open space has been tried at the Commons condominiums, but remains a minor portion of the suburban-style development which has transformed Mendham village and its surrounding farmland into a series of upper-middle-class housing developments.

Mendham's high-style buildings of the past twenty years are derivatives of 20th-century Modernism. This architectural movement, like the earlier Shingle Style, sought to eliminate historical detail from buildings, and use modern materials, such as steel and glass, plastics and plywood. As a result of new building technologies, new forms were possible, free from traditional constraints on height, floor plan, and interior/exterior relationships. Modernism has its roots in European design from between the World Wars, but its influence spread throughout the world and it is also known as the International Style.

MODERN MENDHAM

Right: Oak Knoll Development, Mendham Township

The Oak Knoll subdivision, begun in the mid-1970's, is in a residential area zoned for large lots. While the houses are stylistically varied, the traditional symmetrical five-bay Georgian plan with "colonial" details remains a popular choice.

Below: Kings Ridge Subdivision, Mendham Borough

Several large subdivisions were opened just north of the old village section of Mendham, beginning in the 1960's. This development, with half-acre lots and a standard "builder's colonial" house, approaches the universal housing type of New Jersey's mid-20th century suburban expansion.

MODERN MENDHAM

MODERN MENDHAM

Far Left Above: Platt House

Charles A. Platt, an architect of the New York firm Smotrich and Platt, designed this residence with images of traditional clapboard buildings juxtaposed with Modern architecture. The house received the Architectural Record of Excellence in 1971.

Far Left Below: Lowenstein House

Architect Allan Chimocoff of Princeton, N.J., designed this modern house, completed in 1975. The garden is enlivened with sculptures of family members by Suse Lowenstein.

Left: Contemporary Wooden Residence

Designed by the New York architect Myron Goldfinger, the house was completed in 1980.

Modern, as an architectural style-name, has come to mean buildings constructed from about 1930 to the mid 1970's. The style is identified by the absence of traditional features such as applied ornament and walls with recessed door and window openings. Visual interest in the Modern style is derived from the repetition of geometric modules and the smooth finishes of machined metal, glass and polished wood. The design for a Modern building was often influenced by a concern for energy conservation and an interest in dramatic vistas which required careful site selection and building placement. The Modern style requires skilled workmen, highly finished building materials and carefully selected sites. It is hardly surprising that the time and craftsmanship necessary to achieve the proper look has elevated the style beyond the developer-builder's capabilities.

Each one of Mendham's high-style Modern houses reflects the interests of the architect and his client. They are very different from the vast majority of existing buildings, and are very different from one another. No generalization about the Modern style in Mendham is possible beyond the fact that each is a purposefully new and non-historical design.

MODERN MENDHAM

Right: Audley Manor Chicken House, Talmage Road

In a 1920 book, *Beautiful Homes of Morris County,* which features the area's mansions and estates, the chicken houses of the Talmage Estate, known as Audley Manor, were the only outbuildings to be pictured. The Shingle Style-derivative building, punctuated by a round tower, was renovated in 1981 by the Morristown architectural firm of Nadasky-Kopelson.

Far Right Above: McFarson House, Main Street

This house, built in the center of the village in the 19th century, now shares its residential use with offices on the first floor. The design of the facade displays an unusual feature of local vernacular building — the placement of a three-bay second floor above a five-bay first floor. It is not known why this unique arrangement of windows and door developed, but it may be seen on five buildings in the village.

Far Right Below: Ralston Schoolhouse, Roxiticus Road

Five public school buildings were scattered throughout Mendham in the 19th century, and this one, built of stone, served children in the Ralston area through the 1930's. After the Second World War, it was remodelled into a residence, but the form of the building and the large windows still reveal its original use.

Historical detailing on traditinal building forms has been the preference of the residents of Mendham, and a great many other places, in the second half of the 20th century. This interest in historical architecture is also reflected in the move to restore early buildings. The restoration of America's early buildings since World War II has moved from the home owner's fix-up of a run-down old house to a full-scale discipline involving architects, planners, and specialists in old buildings and their construction. Beginning in the 1960's, saving old buildings, even whole neighborhoods, was seen as a viable alternative to the long-ingrained American habit of tearing down and building new. At first the restoration movement focused on colonial and early American sites, but it now embraces all styles of architecture, and all building types.

Creative re-use of factory buildings, barns, stores, and other utilitarian structures has preserved many buildings which would otherwise have vanished. This type of adaptation has long been practiced, but the reason for such conversions today is not simply to make due in the face of a small budget, but a conscious decision that such structures have worth, and should be preserved.

MODERN MENDHAM

MODERN MENDHAM

In Mendham, many buildings have been preserved and restored. Although there is an impulse to add colonial details to vernacular structures of all dates, there have been some outstanding restoration efforts, preserving Mendham's earliest houses and saving structures which might otherwise have been lost. An old mill serves as a comfortable home, as do two old school houses and a former chicken house. A number of the stores and offices along Main Street were built as houses, and the early store at Ralston is now a museum.

The impulse to preserve these humble structures is as much a romantic attitude toward building as was the 19th-century belief that Gothic ornament would inspire feelings of Christian piety. In the perceived confusion and difficulty of contemporary life, historic buildings seem to give tangible form to the desire for simplicity and order. The enthusiasm for old buildings is an integral part of current architectural taste, and may be counted a characteristic of our time in future architectural histories.

Old buildings, new buildings, original designs, and traditional ornament have all played a part in creating modern Mendham. The desirability of Mendham as a community in which to live is, in part, a result of the balance of all these elements. In recognizing the importance of all styles from the past, and preserving their important characteristics, a visual record of the growth and development of the community is also retained for the enjoyment and education of future generations.

Glossary

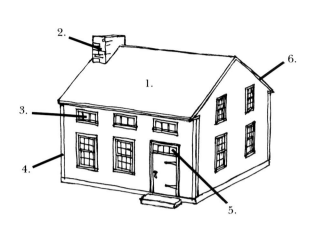

EAST JERSEY COTTAGE

1. Steep gable roof
2. Interior end chimney
3. Eyebrow windows
4. Narrow cornerboards
5. Multi-pane transom
6. Flush eaves

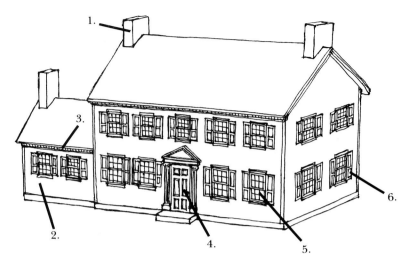

GEORGIAN

1. Interior end chimney
2. Kitchen wing to side
3. Molded cornice
4. Pedimented center entry
5. Multi-light sash
6. Paneled shutters

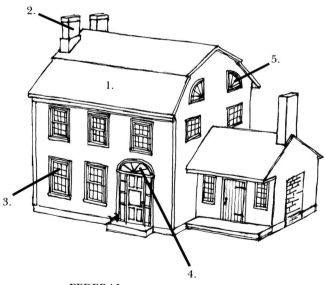

FEDERAL

1. Gambrel roof
2. Paired end chimneys
3. Large windows in molded enframents
4. Fanlight and/or sidelights
5. Quadrant attic windows

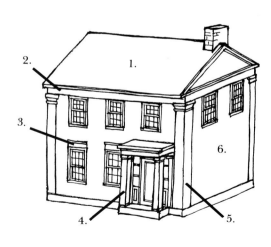

GREEK REVIVAL

1. Low pitch gable roof
2. Wide frieze
3. Entablature over windows
4. Pier supports for entry portico
5. Applied corner pilasters
6. Smooth walls, flushboard of stucco

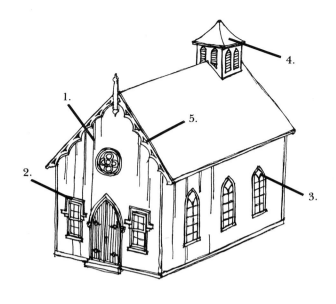

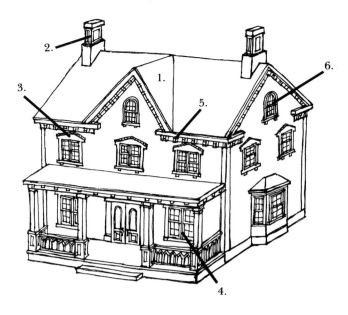

GOTHIC REVIVAL

1. Board and batten siding
2. Hood moldings over square windows
3. Pointed arch windows
4. Turrets or towers
5. Bargeboard

ITALIANATE

1. Cross gable
2. Decorated chimneys
3. Pedimented window lintels
4. Paired windows
5. Bracketed eaves
6. Round arched gable windows

MANSARD

1. Mansard roof
2. Dormers
3. Heavy turned porch supports

QUEEN ANNE

1. Irregular massing including towers and gables
2. Wraparound porch on turned supports
3. Different windows
4. Multiple decorative sidings

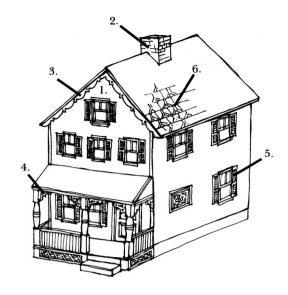

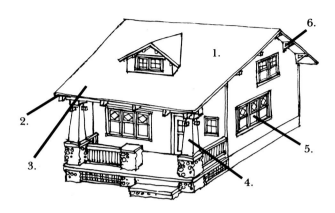

PLANBOOK

1. Gable end facade
2. Narrow chimney
3. Bargeboard
4. Jigsawn ornament on porch
5. Louvered shutters
6. Patterned metal roof

BUNGALOW

1. Low gable roof
2. Extended eaves
3. Integral front porch
4. Sloped porch supports on cobblestone piers
5. Banded windows
6. Knee-brackets

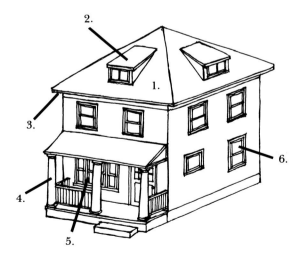

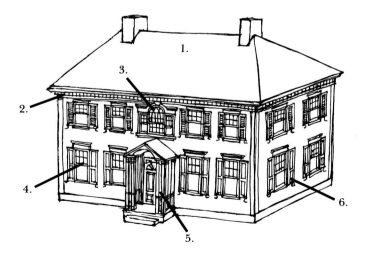

FOURSQUARE

1. Pyramidal roof
2. Shed roof dormers
3. Extended eaves
4. Classical columns on porch
5. Grouped windows
6. Single light sash windows

COLONIAL REVIVAL

1. Hipped roof
2. Ornamental cornice
3. Palladian window
4. Multiple pane over single pane sash
5. Pedimented portico
6. Shutters

Bibliography

GENERAL BIBLIOGRAPHY

Blumenson, John J.-G. *Identifying American Architecture: Pictorial Guide to Styles and Terms 1600-1945*. Nashville: American Association for State and Local History, 1977.

Condit, Carl. *American Building: Materials and Techniques from the First Colonial Settlements to the Present*. Chicago: University of Chicago Press, 1968.

Fitch, James Marston. *American Building 1: The Historical Forces That Shaped It*. 2nd Edition, New York: Schoken, 1973.

Foley, Mary Mix. *The American House*. New York: Harper & Row, 1980.

Handlin, David. *The American Home; Architecture and Society 1815-1915*. Boston: Little, Brown & Company, 1979.

Jordy, William H., and Pierson, William H. Jr. *American Buildings and Their Architects*. Four volumes. New York: Anchor Books, 1976.

McAlester, Virginia, and McAlester, Lee. *A Field Guide to American Houses*. New York: Alfred A. Knopf, 1984.

National Trust for Historic Preservation; Wrenn, Tony P. and Mulloy, Elizabeth. *America's Forgotten Architecture*. New York: Pantheon Press, 1976.

Schwartz, Helen, and Fisher, Margaret Morgan. *The New Jersey House*. New Brunswick, New Jersey: Rutgers University Press, 1983.

Whiffen, Marcus, and Koeper, Frederic. *American Architecture 1607-1976*. Cambridge, Massachusetts: M.I.T. Press, 1981.

Wright, Gwendolyn. *Building the Dream*. New York: Pantheon Books, 1981.

EARLY AMERICAN BUILDING

Cummings, Abbot Lowell. *The Frame Houses of Massachusetts Bay*. Cambridge, Massachusetts: Harvard University Press, 1979.

De Lagerberg, Lars. *New Jersey Architecture, Colonial and Federal*. Springfield, Massachusetts: Walter Whittum, Inc., 1956.

Glassie, Henry. *Pattern in the Material Folk Culture of the Eastern United States*. Philadelphia: University of Pennsylvania Press, 1978.

Kimball, Fiske. *Domestic Architecture of the American Colonies and of the Early Republic*. New York: Dover Publications, Inc., 1980.

Noble, Allen G. *Wood, Brick, and Stone: The North American Settlement Landscape Volume 1: Houses*. Amherst, Mass.: University of Massachusetts Press, 1984.

GREEK REVIVAL ARCHITECTURE

Hamlin, Talbot. *Greek Revival Architecture in America*. New York: Dover Publications, Inc., 1964.

Landy, Jacob. *The Architecture of Minard Lafever*. New York: Columbia University Press, 1970.

Lafever, Minard. *The Modern Builders Guide*. New York: Dover Publications, Inc., 1969.

ITALIANATE AND GOTHIC REVIVAL ARCHITECTURE

Downing, Andrew Jackson. *The Architecture of Country Houses*. New York: Dover Publications, 1969.

————. *Victorian Cottage Residences*. New York: Dover Publications, Inc., 1981.

Stanton, Phoebe. *The Gothic Revival and American Church Architecture*. Baltimore: John Hopkins University Press, 1968.

Vaux, Calvert. *Villas and Cottages*. New York: Dover Publications, Inc., 1970.

BARNS AND MILLS

Noble, Allen G. *Wood, Brick, and Stone: The North American Settlement Landscape. Volume 2: Barns and Farm Structures.* Amherst, Mass.: University of Massachusetts Press, 1984.

Rawson, Richard. *Old Barn Plans.* New York: Bonanza Books, 1979.

Sloan, Eric. *An Age of Barns.* New York: Ballentine Books, 1974.

VICTORIAN ERA ARCHITECTURE

Gottfried, Herbert, and Jennings, Jan. *American Vernacular Design 1870-1940.* New York: Van Nostrand, Reinhold Co., 1985.

The Palliser's Late Victorian Architecture. Reprint of 19th century patternbooks with a new introduction by Michael Tomlan. Watkins Glen, New York: The American Life Foundation, 1978.

THE AGE OF COMFORT

Lancaster, Clay. *The American Bungalow.* New York: Abbeville Press, 1985.

Roth, Leland. *McKim, Mead, and White Architects.* New York: Harper & Row, 1983.

Scully, Vincent. *The Shingle Style and the Stick Style.* Rev. ed. New Haven: Yale University Press, 1971.

Stickley, Gustav. *Craftsman Homes* and *More Craftsman Homes.* New York: Dover Publications, Inc., 1982.

MODERN ARCHITECTURE

Frampton, Kenneth. *Modern Architecture: A Critical History.* New York: Oxford University Press, 1980.

Mumford, Lewis, editor. *Roots of Contemporary American Architecture.* New York: Dover Publications, Inc. 1972.

Scully, Vincent. *Modern Architecture.* New York: George Braziller, 1975.

Index

Page numbers in italic indicate illustrations